# BEGIN IT NOW

COMPILED BY
PEACE MITCHELL
KATY GARNER

Women Changing the World Press acknowledges the Elders and Traditional owners of country throughout Australia and their connection to lands, waters and communities. We pay our respect to Elders past and present and extend that respect to all Aboriginal and Islander peoples today. We honour more than sixty thousand years of Indigenous women's voices, stories, leadership and wisdom.

Copyright © Peace Mitchell and Katy Garner
First published in Australia in 2025
by Women Changing the World Press
an imprint of KMD Books
Waikiki, WA 6169

All rights reserved. No part of this book may be used or reproduced by any means, graphic, electronic or mechanical, including photocopying, recording, taping or by any information storage retrieval system without the written permission of the copyright owner except in the case of brief quotations embodied in critical articles and reviews.

Because of the dynamic nature of the Internet, any web addresses or links contained in this book may have changed since publication and may no longer be valid. The views expressed in this work are solely those of the author and do not necessarily reflect the views of the publisher and the publisher hereby disclaims any responsibility for them.

Typeset in Adobe Garamond Pro 12/17pt

 A catalogue record for this work is available from the National Library of Australia

National Library of Australia Catalogue-in-Publication data:
Begin it Now/Peace Mitchell and Katy Garner

ISBN:
978-1-7643726-0-2
(Paperback)

*"Whatever you can do, or dream you can, begin it; Boldness has genius, power, and magic in it." Johann Wolfgang von Goethe*

*We dedicate this book to the women of the world ready to step out and chase their dreams. It's our time and we're ready! Let's begin it now!*

# CONTENTS

Introduction – Peace Mitchell ................................................................................. 1

Goldilocks & My Glorious Gut – Aaila Greene ..................................................... 7

Burundi Was Just the Beginning – Alicia Nukuri ................................................ 25

Dance With Uncertainty – Amanda Mullin .......................................................... 33

Letters To My Younger Self – Anna Abesadze ..................................................... 47

Steel Caps, Stilettos & Stuff They Said I Couldn't Do – Gina Field .................. 61

To Live Fully In Each Moment – Jessica Hansen ................................................ 73

The Power Of The First Step – Laura Muirhead .................................................. 87

The Power Of Starting – Laurelle Jno Baptiste .................................................... 99

From Refugee To Humanitarian – Le Thu Phan-Tran ...................................... 111

Rising From Rock Bottom – Parvina Mirakhmedova ....................................... 127

A Journey From Desperation To Passion – Rand Alkishtaini .......................... 141

The Fifty-Dollar Awakening – Rania Al Khusaibi ............................................. 151

The Human Power – Romaa Rajadhyaksha ....................................................... 167

Before I Forget – Saode Savary ............................................................................. 181

Beginnings In Chaos – Sarah Macrae .................................................................. 199

Who I Was Meant To Be – Sharon Swietek ........................................................ 209

The Power Of Following Your Heart & Starting Over – Sinja Hallam ........... 221

From Silence To Shining – Stella Olivia Kikoyo ................................................ 239

Mountains Of Laundry – Susan Toft .................................................................... 255

# INTRODUCTION

## PEACE MITCHELL

It's your time and you are ready. Begin, start today, let yourself make mistakes, be imperfect, make a mess of it … but just start!

Stop holding yourself back or waiting for the right time, the right circumstances, the right moment or for everything to be perfect. There will never be a better time to start than right now!

I spoke to someone recently who had been sitting on an idea for ten years. The idea had stayed with them faithfully for all that time. It was a brilliant idea, she said. It was going to be so incredible, she told me. But she hadn't done anything with it … and she couldn't tell me what it was because she was worried that if she started doing it or even speaking about it, someone would steal her idea. So instead of having her idea out in the world, she simply did nothing. For ten years!

The fear of her idea being stolen was holding her back from taking action. Wanting to protect her plans, at all cost, meant she couldn't move forward on her dreams … and sadly, probably never would.

I met another person who really wanted to get their idea off the ground. They wanted to start and see what would happen. They had big dreams and big plans, but it was as if they were frozen. They even spent years writing meticulous business plans, doing course after course and investing hours (weeks and months and years) into yet more study. All the while, dreaming of one day gracing the catwalks of Paris, yet doing little to make that happen.

For this person, fear of not being ready was keeping her stuck, spinning her wheels on getting started on her dream. Taking course after course in the hope of one day feeling worthy enough, or qualified enough, to start, is a common way fear keeps us from taking that first step towards our dreams.

I've held myself back from taking action in the past too. My sister and I had dreamt of having a global brand long before we launched one. We even hired a business coach to help us develop the strategy. Unfortunately, the advice we received was terrible. Instead of helping us to create a plan for world expansion, he squashed our dreams and told us to stay small and 'just focus on Australia'. Telling us 'Why be a small fish in a big pond, when you could be a big fish in a small pond?' Instead of giving us advice and strategy, he projected his own fears and memories of his own past failures on to us!

His advice, and the fear it came with, kept us stuck and small for far longer than if we'd had the support and encouragement of someone with a global perspective and an open mind.

If only we'd had the courage to give it a try back then. I often wonder what our business, community and impact would look like if we'd had the courage and support to start our global brand sooner.

I know it wasn't just the coach though. At other times in our business journey, I've been hesitant to try new things unless *I was 100% certain* that they were going to work. I found myself preferring to stick to tried and tested products and services we'd offered before that we knew our audience would want. This was great because we knew what worked but it held us back from trying new things.

Underneath that reluctance for trying new things was my fear of failure. Especially public failure, where everyone would know we'd failed - like when an event had to be cancelled because we didn't sell enough tickets. How embarrassing! How humiliating! How would I ever survive something like that? As ridiculous as that sounds, this is what my fears would tell me. My fear saw any mistakes, or lack of perfection, in every way as a sure sign of failure and public disgrace, trying to keep me safe by making sure I never took risks or tried new things.

Fortunately for us, we met someone who told us she treated her business like science. She said that when she was launching a new idea, project or campaign, she would treat it like an experiment. If she launched something new that didn't work, instead of feeling humiliated, she would get curious, take the time to uncover why it hadn't worked, then tweak things and try again.

She explained that she didn't worry about making mistakes along the way. Because in her experience, mostly when something failed, maybe a few people would notice it had happened, but usually people are so busy working on their own projects they wouldn't notice. And those that did would move on with their life and forget about it. It was only us who were up at night thinking about it.

This approach was life changing for us ... and so freeing. Instead of feeling held back by fear of failure and the pressure of always being perfect, we approached new ideas and initiatives as if they were an experiment.

We've been running international business expansion tours for six years now, but the first time we promoted one we had no idea if anyone would book in. We decided that if no-one else booked in, we would just go to London by ourselves anyway ... and have a great time. This mindset shift instantly took the pressure off. The trip ended up being a huge success with eight other women joining us in Lisbon and London for our first tour.

Fear holds us all back in a multitude of ways; fear of not knowing enough, not knowing how, not being enough, fear of failure, fear of making a mistake, fear of not being ready, fear of imperfection, fear of other people taking our ideas, not to mention other people projecting their fear onto us ... and the list goes on and on. Fear is what's often underneath *not taking action* on the life of our dreams, bringing our visions to life and being all that we can be. Fear is keeping us from dreaming, planning and sometimes even beginning.

But it doesn't have to be this way. If we can overcome our fear and take that first step towards the life of our dreams, we can start to discover what's possible for us!

I've learnt that one minute can change your life and when I'm being held back by fear I remind myself that I can do anything for one minute.

It had been many years since I'd done yoga. I wanted to try it again and develop a daily practice. Going straight into a thirty-minute session seemed overwhelming when it had been so long but I really wanted to try it out and overcome my fear of quitting because I wasn't able to do it *perfectly*.

So, I got creative. I made a plan to commit to a daily yoga session, at home, every day for thirty days.

But I also decided I was going to treat it like an experiment, making it fun and easy. I promised myself if I missed a day, or did anything imperfectly, I was going to forgive myself and try again the next day. The most surprising thing I did though, was to commit to just one minute of yoga on the first day, then exactly two minutes on the second day, three minutes on the third day and so on, until I got to day thirty.

My friends looked at me like I was crazy and laughed out loud!

'You're going to do just one minute of yoga! What's the point of that?' they asked.

But I did it anyway, and thirty days later they still weren't doing daily yoga, but I was!

My plan had worked. I was so amazed! I had the courage to begin, even though I wasn't ready, even though I couldn't do it perfectly. Even though I started with such small steps. After three days I started looking forward to it. After a week it had become a habit. After two weeks I noticed I was starting to get better at the poses. After three weeks I noticed I was getting stronger and fitter. In the end I did over one hundred days of yoga! And it all began with just one minute of courage and letting go of my fears.

In this book, you'll hear the stories of remarkable women from around the world who have had the courage to overcome their fears and take action in beginning something new and exciting!

So, what are you waiting for? Whatever it is, start where you are, with what you have. It's time to begin it now!

# GOLDILOCKS & MY GLORIOUS GUT

## (MY MAGICAL CRUSADE TO A BRAND-NEW LIFE)

### AAILA GREENE

**NOW**

I love order.

Polished bits tied up with sexy, little bows.

That's what I dreamed of for you with this chapter – a story so perfect, it makes Marie Kondo look like a slacker.

But that's not what's happening here.

Welcome to the trenches of my life … in real time. Like a circus - but where the animals take over and parade down the street in drag - as I follow my pain-in-the-butt inner voice which *refuses* to shut up, and bosses me around like I'm its human spawn.

So, if you want me to pitch you a 'follow your intuition' path that's Insta sexy, posted in my bikini, drinking Mai Tais in the Caribbean (whilst being massaged by a rockstar with hot abs) … spoiler alert, you won't be finding that magical unicorn here.

What you will find however is the down 'n dirty story of how I obsessively started following my intuition and how it – legit - *changed everything.*

But wait … I'm getting ahead of myself. Let's rewind to where this cray-cray story began:

With Goldie and my glorious gut.

## SUNNY COAST, QUEENSLAND – TWO YEARS AGO

I'm in a Mexican stand-off with my intuition. It's day ten, it's not going well, and I think we both know who's gonna win.

"MOVE TO CAIRNS."

On rotation, about 40,000 times a day, at 20,000 decibels in my mind.

I've tried every type of denial, including eating my body weight in crisps, but it won't stop.

After ten days of this parasitic mantra taking over my brain, I finally tap out of the ring. You win. I'm listening … please just stop!

I drag my half deranged, sleep deprived body into bed and crawl under the covers. Faaaaaaaark. I hold tight to my snuggle pillow as I let the fear wash over me. This voice isn't telling me to have a week in the tropics taking selfies with ludicrously ginormous dinosaur birds. It's telling me to pack up my *whole* life – the life I've meticulously spent the last six years building … and let it all go.

My friends, community, home. Everything.

Tears and snot are pouring down my face in a fear-grief super-sized combo that would make that sexy massaging rockstar run away … very far away.

But I let them fall cos there's nothing left to do now but sit with what I've been avoiding.

"MOVE TO CAIRNS."

My intuition is a sneaky supersleuth rascal that's pinned me in a head lock. Since surviving a year of hand rehab, losing 90% of my friends and an agonising Titanic style love-of-my-life heartbreak, I *finally* promised (half whimpering on my knees) to follow my intuition … *no matter what.*

# BEGIN IT NOW

Not when I can be bothered. Not when it's easy. No. Matter. What.

I desperately want a free pass from my promise. An etheric spirit lawyer to lovingly rock me while feeding me chocolate, saying, 'no worries sweetheart. If it's too hard for you honey pot, just don't go.'

But my intuition is like the mafia – and you know you can't mess with those babies, cos if you try, you'll end up in a Tarantino film.

My terror-exorcism goes on for six hours involving fourteen tissues, three rounds of sobbing, some hyena hysterical laughing and finally … *peace*.

To be fair to my intuition – I'm like that horse that won't leave the stall. The one that cheers on the other horses, saying, 'Great canter!' while I sit pretty, punching down sugar cubes. This is the part where you might be surprised to find out I'm a professional psychic channel (yep - think festivals, hotlines and wellness centres). And giving guidance for *other* people has been the most fulfilling part of my life for decades.

But since guidance for my *own* life is frequently both unpleasant and inconvenient, I've adopted a pick'n'mix style of listening:

Follow when easy.

Ignore when scary.

My intuition is calling bluff with my BS pretence of listening and rips my charade to shreds like a cat with the weekend paper.

Three months ago, it guided me to train in Astro Maps, showing how everyone has unique locations to thrive for career, love and a happy home life. And that was my last snot fest.

Cos that's when I find out that for six years (as my life implodes in *every* area), I've been living on my Chiron line - Core Wounds - like a day spa in sulphuric acid. Except it's my life – hence the snot.

My intuition knows I hate change. But it also knows I love truth and don't enjoy spas in sulphuric acid. So – it uses this hectic little Chiron line to hint that, soon, my butt will be dragged away, in search of a new community and life.

My inner Goldilocks has just been activated and *home gurl* is looking for new digs. And while my intuition knows that almost *any* line is gonna be better than a Chiron line, it sweetens the deal, sending me to my rainbow magic Jupiter line promising luck, success and happiness on drip feed.

And so, the adventure *begins* …

## FAR NORTH QUEENSLAND

I spend six weeks following my intuitive mafia's demands:

Give away life-time's possessions – check.

Sobbingly say goodbye to shrapnel of remaining friends – check.

Hold onto small skerrick of faith – half check.

After my seventeen-hour road trip North, I'm gently welcomed to Far North Queensland by two cyclones.

I almost pee my pants at the town meeting when serious-looking uniformed people talk evacuation plans and the need for radios as life-lines (like the 80s but with more wind).

Luckily by this stage, my intuition's filled me in on its dirty little secret:

I'm not *staying* in Far North Queensland. Instead, I'm about to be taken on a blow-by-blow ride through my psyche, battling demons across the country before getting spat out as a digital nomad in some random unknown land.

It's as enticing as a lobotomy in Hell.

I desperately cling to this prehistoric new land where crocs and cassowaries roam like nobody's business. It's 4 billion degrees with 5 million percent humidity, but good luck having a swim. Box jelly fish and invisible mini jellies are primed to maim and kill … and crocs are ready for snacks.

# BEGIN IT NOW

I hate change. My neurodiverse brain loves systems and rituals. I ache for a new home where I can just be, with people who see and love me. My sneaky intuition used FNQ as bait to get me out of Chiron Hell. But as much as I *want* it to feel right, my inner Goldilocks is shaking her annoying little head.

My eight months in FNQ are a live impact drill to crush my fear of change. All prior rules about life evaporate instantly. My neighbour canoes down our post cyclone street (now doubling as a river) as a cassowary strolls past my letter box.

FNQ people are a whole other kind of chill. I figure they face so many things that can instantly wipe them, that they're like a living, breathing community of Zen monks. Chillax honey. No cyclones. Not a croc snack. Not headbutted by a cassowary (that's a thing btw). Winning.

I shake my head at the pseudo-Zen monks around me. I landed as a 10 on the stress-my-box-off meter, but I'm leaving as a 6. (Note: FNQ people are a 0).

But right after my inner Goldie tells me I'm leaving, I make the kind of friend I've been yearning for, for years. *Finally*, a human I feel real with, who sees and knows my heart, with the same crazed belly laugh and psychic juju. Beneath a mountain of oracle cards, tea and childlike giggles, we dream up our mutual vision of being speakers on cruise ships and global events. And we promise to reunite at an event in a sunset spa, mocktail *in hand*!

Daaaaaaam! Every part of me wants to tell Goldie and my intuition where they can stick their demands, as I tearily cling to my new friend, triple hugging her goodbye.

But like The Fairy Godmother with Cinderella (#joykill), Goldie's waiting and she has a plan. Next stop - my other Aussie Jupiter spot - The Central Coast, NSW (27 hours' drive south.)

# AAILA GREENE

## CENTRAL COAST, NSW

I rent a room living with an arty academic and settle into my new Jupiter chapter (Part 2: The Revenge). Three to five months, Goldie says. By this stage I know resistance is futile, so with a whiteboard the size of Brazil, feeling disturbingly like Russel Crow from *A Beautiful Mind*, I hatch a plan.

I'm half possessed redoing my cv and Jupiter the Revenge goes off! I get two jobs; one as festival volunteer coordinator for the local LGBTIQA+ festival and another running LGBTIQA+ youth support groups. I get funding to run a community workshop on how to make workplaces queer friendly and spend hundreds of hours setting up and launching my website.

Workwise, it's like getting dipped in nectar, with a hive of bees pollinating their bits off in the garden that is me. But I completely ignore a nearby Pluto/Lilith line (think - destruction and inner scream sandwich) that's been brewing a level 10 gut punch and is ready to blow.

A few years ago, when I stopped people pleasing and upped my boundaries and self-respect, my relationships started an RIP pile up. It's been a revolving door, watching person after person exit, and agonising that so few are willing or able to continue life with the new me.

I look homeless, my butt is welded to the couch and I'm obsessively rereading the text from Hell. It's from the only family member I have regular contact with, and a voice deep inside me is screaming NO. Not one more time. I don't care what happens. I don't care if I lose everyone. NOT ONE MORE TIME!

I can't give them what they want. I can't keep being punished for being myself and I know not even Mad Max can save us this time. The Pluto Lilith gut punch comes through sharp and cold. They cut me. Like a fly at a BBQ, I'm evicted from the relationship and my social phobia goes from 10 to 200.

# BEGIN IT NOW

I can barely see. I'm spiralling in a tunnel of revolving pastel colours as I grasp hard not to slide into pure blackness. I SOS my closest friend and sob cry my raw pain in biblical wails.

I'm broken. Destroyed. Barely able to eat or move.

But my mate Jupiter is stunt-doubling as my saviour. With volunteers to schedule, groups to run and a pending date with power-point, falling apart isn't an option.

And that's when my flat mate tells me she's selling the house, and I need to move.

Mic drop.

No judgement if you wanna sack my intuition crew for negligence and incompetence. It definitely looks like they've dropped the ball.

But a voice inside speaks softly; 'You came here to give your family one last try. Now - Let. Them. Go.' Boooft!

Goldie's a hard NO to renting another room in this town. So, I wrap up my work commitments, say goodbye to my beautiful, kind LGBTIQA+ contacts and head to my next stop, as per Goldie and my intuitive ball 'n chain - the Far South Coast.

## FAR SOUTH COAST, NSW

Hot off my generational trauma purge, my intuition crew wants to check if I've *really* broken my '*I'll do anything if you love me*' pattern, so they plant a fabulous spawn; my new flat mate.

Within minutes of arriving, I wanna tap out of the ring cos this puppy is playing to win. For two weeks, the problems are stacking up like Jenga gone wrong. The spices I use, the way I cook, my hair gel, the way I set up my room. Everything I do is a problem and when I try to share that I'm struggling with her micromanagement, she has a fantastic solution – eviction! I avoid the temptation to push tiny sticks into her eyeballs. Instead, I pack my car and decide life as a hermit, avoiding all humans forever, is a total genius plan.

I check my maps in the area and boom – Saturn Pluto. *Control* and *destruction*. May as well have dropped a grenade into that house and thrown the pin. But I'm proud of myself. It'd be easy to be 'nice'. To twist myself into a pretzel day after day so she likes me. But I hold onto my right to *be me*, to *speak up* … and pass the test!

My intuition crew are high-fiving and dancing the samba.

And that's when I get an email about a workshop in Melbourne … at 10am tomorrow … and a parade of unicorns starts jumping on my face. 'GO. GO. GO!' Goldie and crew are flipping their lids.

So, after a seven-hour drive, the next morning, I'm at the workshop and a woman made of pure sunshine starts chatting. After a day sharing mutually-moving, raw, real-life stories, she hands me the keys to her spare apartment *as a base* 'while I'm here.'

She seems sane. And has concluded after a day of heartfelt teary shares that I'm not a psycho who'll graffiti her feature wall and pee in her sock drawers.

So, I do the only logical thing one can when the universe throws you a bone the size of The Ganges. I take it. And my sexy Inner-City Melbournian is born.

Note: Evidence is starting to build that my intuition and Goldie are indeed supreme legends of Galactic proportions (um, your honour, please withdraw all prior comparisons of my intuition to the mafia, ball n chain etc.)

## MELBOURNE, VICTORIA

I'm dropped into the LGBTIQA+ hub of Collingwood Melbourne and my Mars and Ceres lines (*work* and *happy home*) have me frothing. Sapphic speed dating events, LGBT friendly everything (including a rainbow pavement at the top of my street) and it's raining pubs, cafes, comedy and world class live music.

I go to a social change conference and am inspired by a whole other type of human and life. People who *do* stuff. Not scared bunnies like me who *wanna* do stuff but eat chocolate instead. These people are legit changing the world and I decide it's time for me to start learning by osmosis. I run the first round of my online intuition programs and life feels exciting, like anything is possible.

And that's when Goldie and my intuitive mafia crew step in like the joy killers they are. 'Reduce your life to two suitcases in prep for overseas. Training ground – New Zealand.'

I break into a sweat. NOOOOOOO!

But my apartment stay is nearly up and so, three days later, I land a five week housesit on a 100-acre deer farm in New Zealand, kicking off in a week. It's 50 minutes from my favourite place on earth (Lake Tekapo) and Goldie is dry screaming a hard YES!

I frantically spend my last week in Melbourne trying not to punch the scales, as I reduce my life's possessions to two suitcases, 24 kg and a ticket out of Oz.

## SOUTH ISLAND, NEW ZEALAND

New Zealand greets me with three dogs, eight chickens, 200 deer and a bull that bellows like a drooling, hairy grim reaper. Life on the farm involves collecting eggs, gazing at deer, writing and staying Switzerland-neutral with the political war cries between the indoor and outdoor dogs.

I have Mercury and Venus lines here for *Inspired communication* and *love*! Woot woot! I start sharing on Insta and *love* creating these mini videos about life on the farm. The crazy bulls are a hit. I'm blogging, writing a book (the full guts'n glory version of *this* story) and my heart feels blessed and content. Like love is just sitting on the land here wrapping me in non-stop hugs.

I drive to Lake Tekapo and spend hours staring at turquoise perfection and Alpine wildflowers. I LOVE the land. I LOVE the people (Goldie is starting to froth). But we appear to have hit a snag with New Zealand South Island weather.

For a Queenslander, happy in temperatures above 20 degrees Celsius, the New Zealand South Island poses a small hiccup to Goldie's long-term joy. And by hiccup, I mean it decimates it.

It's mid-Summer and it's been raining for three weeks, with vector angles defying physics. It's 7 degrees with gorillas-in-the-mist fog threatening to bury my soul and all hope for joy. I'm wearing every layer I own, am using three hot water bottles and am thinking about sleeping with the dogs in the kennel for body heat.

The sun comes out, I rip my clothes off like an Eskimo in Hell and start dancing on the lawn in half-crazed manic joy. The chickens are sunbaking and I'm so happy, I nearly weep. Until four hours later, when the clouds bury the sun as though it had never existed and may never exist again.

Goldie stares at me with a horrified, bewildered face.

I hear you babe.

But it's cracking my brain cos it's *so* beautiful and feels *amazing*. So, I take a road trip to Hanmer Springs and Kaikoura to see if Goldie gets a YES, despite the arctic climate.

I absolutely LOVE both places, but *nothing* is flowing. It's like the antiflow … if that's a thing.

And that's when I see the extra line my optimism-denial combo missed: Saturn. Think fun police. (#joykillonroids). This homeboy sends obstacles to help you get real and sort your life. I'd like to evict him from the galaxy.

In two days, I have to leave my housesit and I have *no* idea what to do. *What if I'm wrong? What if I'm crazy?* I let the tears fall. Maybe it's all a waste of time. Maybe I'll never find a home or tribe and I'm destined to wander the globe alone forever (settle down Aaila, settle down).

Finally, I take a tea break from my mini break-down and that's when my intuition says slowly, calmly and clearly: 'GO HOME.'

Where to?

'SUNNY COAST.'

And then it hits me. Much to my severe denial, my tiny house is waiting to be renovated and prepped for sale (along with twenty equally repugnant tasks I shoved deep into Pandora's box before I left).

I swallow hard as I feel Goldie nod a quiet YES. Saturn high-fives and puts up a 10.

And just like that - Saturn kicks my butt out of my NZ love bubble – back to the sulphur spa where it all began.

## SUNNY COAST – THE RETURN

I land back on the Sunny Coast and immediately strike housesit gold: Infinity pool, rolling deck, breathtaking views and absolute silence. #wheredoisign

After checking the maps, I see my landing is timed with Lucky Jupiter flying right over the Sunny Coast and I'm so happy, I'm literally dance-crying half-naked on the deck.

What if my intuition kicked me out of NZ cos *this* was waiting for me?

What if some things don't flow so that other things *do*? Woah!

I feel like Buddha. But I know that Saturn would be pissed if I use the next four months to *only* work on my tan and Netflix playlist.

So – I decide to follow the Saturn butt-kick vibe and use this gift as a base to run the full set of my intuition programs. And, for four months (amongst naked swims, sunbaking and kilos of cacao), I'm a diligent little work banana and start a happy throuple with Jupiter and Saturn.

#weridestlovetriangleever

A quiet confidence is building as I turn up for myself and my students, week after week. No matter what life brings, I'm experiencing the 'chop wood, carry water' of doing what needs to be done, as best I can.

I find out I'm a finalist in the Women Changing the World Awards, get offered a place in *this* book and my life is transforming before my eyes. I'm teary when I find out some one in FNQ nominated me for the awards cos if I hadn't followed Goldie and my intuitive crew, *you* wouldn't be reading this now. Not everything makes sense at the time, but maybe it makes sense in the end.

Housesit over, programs complete – now – it's time to *finally* do what I came here to do!

## SUNNY COAST – LIFT OFF INTO THE WORLD

The transition from my mansion into my tiny house is brutal and I lose a week in a chocolate-denial haze. I'm in my fam's back yard. They call me family and I'm practicing letting them love me and loving them as best I can. I have a fresh Bunnings order sitting on the bench and I'm finally facing the music I came here to do. Goldie's still looking for a home, but we're more patient and trust the timing. It's coming. And my bucket list of dream countries and experiences is looking up at me like a happy bunny cos it knows that in a few months, I'm leaving Australia to find my soul fam and new life.

I wanted my life to look 'shinier' when finishing this chapter. I'm not a social media sensation and still have no 'guarantee' that the gut messages I've been receiving over the last few years will reap any flashy looking awards.

But I *know* they're making me the *best* me and bringing me my *best* life.

Playing life like a safe scaredy cat was ACT 1. Following my gut is

# BEGIN IT NOW

ACT 2. It sends me into a cold sweat most days, but every win shows me I'm on track. Like Spring, tiny buds are blooming and I can almost smell them opening.

Listening to Goldie and her crew, constantly adapting to every place, changed me. And I know it's prepping me for what's coming.

Cos I'm your self-appointed unicorn-angel cheer leader, helping *you* do what you came here to do by following *your* gut.

There'll be buckets of tears and a slayed heart.

There'll be moments on your knees, begging to tap out.

You'll want to head butt your intuition team into Pandora's box and hand the key to Hades.

But – no matter what your life looks like along the way, or what others think, *you'll* know who you are. And peace, love and joy will pour into your world. Cos when you follow your gut, *everything* changes.

Not one person on Earth knows what you need more than you. You're the Jedi master you've been waiting for. Your soul is connected to *everything*, *aching* to deliver your most delicious, ecstatic life.

Catch is – you gotta listen *and* act. And sometimes, it's gonna rip you a new one.

But what if you're the superhero the world needs? Your song, your words, your heart? You'll only know if you press pause from the noise and follow the most important voice on the planet – your gut.

*Not when you have time. Not when life is less stressful.*

*NOW.* Your life is a gift. So go share your magnificence with the world.

And do it – *now.*

# AAILA GREENE

A 2025 Finalist in the Women Changing the World Awards, Aaila Greene has spent the last 25 years mentoring good-hearted rebels to listen to their souls & live authentic lives. Born psychic, with a background in Psychology, Life Coaching, Astrology & Nature-based Ceremony, she developed her own style of Intuition Coaching, supporting people to access their Genius /inner voice and live fulfilling, joy-filled, extraordinary lives.

With a decade as a performing singer-songwriter, active blocks in eco-activism/permaculture & immersions in indigenous ceremony (in Australia, Mexico, Bolivia & Peru), Aaila knows that life is rarely simple but loves how it all weaves together in the end.

Her greatest vision is to inspire a Soul Living movement where millions of good-hearted rebels courageously live from their souls, creating an authentic 'loving kindness' tipping point on earth. Founder of INTUITION THE GAME, she playfully & cheekily helps people live out-of-the-box lives, on their own terms, from a spirit of love & collaboration.

As a passionate environmentalist and part of the LGBTIQA+ community, she also helps Artists, Activists & Leaders follow their intuition

# AAILA GREENE

& live their truest, most inspiring versions of life. This is how she changes the world – by inspiring visionaries to live their missions, one beautiful soul at a time.

Aaila is wild, loving & practices what she preaches, using astro-cartography (astro maps) to travel the world & explore different cultures, activating every part of her soul. She's constantly awestruck by the magic of life, the kindness of people and the magnificent, raw beauty of the planet. Her happy places are laying in the sun, nature gazing, kale chips, gliding through water, wild dancing and belly laughs with people she loves.

Website: aailagreene.com

# BURUNDI WAS JUST THE BEGINNING

## ALICIA NUKURI

There's a moment in every story when the dust settles, and you realise the beginning wasn't the end, it was the ignition. Mine started in a slum called Bwiza, in the heart of Africa, in Burundi. But this isn't a story about staying there. It's about rising, crossing borders and becoming someone I never imagined I could be.

I want you to feel this with me, not just read it. I want you to walk through the narrow alleyways of my childhood, hear the silence after gunfire, and then feel the rush of wind as I take flight across continents. Because if you've ever felt stuck, broken or invisible, I want you to know beginnings don't define you; it's what you do next that does.

**THE SOUND OF SURVIVAL**

I was born in 1999, in a one-bedroom house where five of us lived shoulder to shoulder. Bwiza wasn't just poor, it was loud with struggle. I remember the sound of soldiers barging into our home, the crack of gunfire, the roar of planes overhead. Hunger was a daily visitor. My father, a taxi driver, did everything he could to feed us. My mother, battling a mental illness, often turned violent. Inside and outside, the world felt unsafe.

But even then, something inside me whispered – 'Hold on.'

When I moved to my grandmother's house at six, it felt like stepping into a new chapter. The walls were sturdier. The nights were quieter. My father remarried, and my stepmother, working in humanitarian aid, made sure I went to school. That was the first time I tasted hope.

*Lesson 1: Resilience is a decision.*

Even when life feels like chaos, you can choose to hold on. You can choose to believe that something better is coming.

## A PASSPORT TO POSSIBILITY

At eleven, my stepmother got a job in Burkina Faso. We packed up our lives and flew west. Suddenly, I was in a French school, surrounded by students who had never known war. I soaked up every lesson like sunlight. Then came Moldova, Eastern Europe, and an American school that felt like a dream. I had a motto - *Education will get me out of poverty.* And I knew it with all my heart.

I graduated with honours. I was ready to fly higher.

*Lesson 2: Education is liberation.*

It's not just about books; it's about unlocking doors you don't even know exist. It's about rewriting your story.

## THE STORM WITHIN

In 2018, I landed in Montreal for university. Everything was going well ... until it wasn't. I started feeling heavy, like a thundercloud had settled over my head. The trauma I thought I'd buried came rushing back. The violence, the hunger, the fear - it all returned, louder than ever.

I was diagnosed with a mental illness. Depression wrapped itself around me like a fog. I felt like I was fighting invisible forces. But then I remembered something; I had survived worse.

I reached out for help. I returned to Africa. I saw mental health professionals. I took medication. But more than that, I changed my mindset. I reminded myself that healing was part of the journey.

*Lesson 3: Healing is not weakness.*

Asking for help isn't giving up, it's gearing up. It's choosing to fight with better tools.

## THE CLIMB BACK UP

In 2023, I resumed my studies in South Africa. I had taken a break, but I wasn't broken. I was rebuilding. And this time, I was stronger. I started achieving things I once thought impossible. I was working, studying and preparing to travel again. My childhood had taught me to be a fighter. Now I was becoming a builder.

*Lesson 4: Your past does not define your future.*

It shapes you, yes. But it doesn't limit you. You get to decide what comes next.

## THE POWER OF REPRESENTATION

Today, I look back and see a girl who survived war, crossed continents, battled depression and rose again. I represent more than myself, I represent every child who grew up in chaos and dared to dream. I represent resilience, hope and the power of transformation.

*Lesson 5: Representation matters.*

When you rise, you carry others with you. Your story becomes a bridge for someone else.

## WHAT I WANT YOU TO REMEMBER

Burundi was just the beginning. And maybe your beginning was hard too. But here's what I want you to walk away with:

- Resilience is a decision. You can choose to rise.

- Education is liberation. It opens doors.
- Healing is not weakness. It's strength in motion.
- Your past does not define your future. You do.
- Representation matters. Your story can light the way for others.

So, wherever you are right now, whether you're in the middle of your storm or just stepping into the light. I want you to know, you are not alone. And this is not the end … it's just the beginning.

# ALICIA NUKURI

My name is Alicia Nukuri, and I was born in Burundi, a country that taught me the meaning of resilience before I even understood the word. Growing up in a slum called Bwiza, surrounded by conflict and hardship, I learned early on that survival was not just physical, it was mental, emotional, and spiritual. My journey has taken me across continents, from West Africa to Eastern Europe, North America to Southern Africa, and each step has shaped the woman I've become.

Education has always been my anchor. It was my way out of poverty, my way forward, and my way up. I've studied in some of the best schools across the globe, and today I'm proud to be a member of the Golden Key International Honour Society, a recognition given to high-achieving university students worldwide. That honor reminds me that no matter where you start, excellence is always within reach.

I've faced my share of storms including mental health challenges that nearly broke me but I chose healing. I chose growth. And I chose to turn my pain into purpose.

Today, I advocate for African talent, represent voices that deserve to be heard, and build bridges between cultures. My work spans fashion, sports, and education, but at the heart of it all is a deep desire to empower others.

## ALICIA NUKURI

I write this chapter not just to share my story, but to remind you that your beginning doesn't define your ending. If you've ever felt unseen, unheard, or underestimated, I hope my journey shows you that you are capable of rising and that your voice matters!

# DANCE WITH UNCERTAINTY

## AMANDA MULLIN

There is a moment that stays with me. Two years into business, standing in the quiet of my newly opened second location; floor-to-ceiling windows framing Sydney Harbour, that blue, blue Australian sky, sunlight spilling across fresh paint. I'd poured everything into getting here - a career change in my thirties, eight years completing my doctorate while raising our family, risking our savings on a dream.

For weeks, this view had filled my heart with pure joy. Proof that the hard work was worth it. Evidence I could scale what I'd built. I was already dreaming about locations three, four and five.

But that morning, standing at those windows, something felt different. My body felt different. The fatigue that had been creeping up on me for months – the way my lunchtime runs had become impossible, the way I'd wake up exhausted – suddenly felt impossible to ignore.

I had an appointment with a specialist that afternoon.

## HOW MY DREAM TOOK SHAPE

Like many women, my business began with a passion to create change.

As a clinical psychologist, I'd grown frustrated with how our industry approached mental health. Therapy was hidden away in dark, windowless rooms – spaces that seemed to reinforce shame and stigma rather than healing.

I wanted something different. A practice filled with light and warmth. A welcoming space founded on uncompromising clinical excellence, where science-based treatments were delivered with genuine care. Where seeking help felt like an act of courage and self-care wasn't something to hide.

That vision became my first practice.

The early days were intoxicating. That first client walking through the doors. Watching our appointment books fill. The deep satisfaction of building something meaningful … from nothing. Within months, I'd outgrown my initial space, found a dream location and began hiring staff. By year two, I'd expanded into our second location with a team of nearly twenty. I dreamt of a national network of practices transforming mental health care.

We had strong systems, values-led leadership, a loyal client base, long waitlists, industry recognition, awards on the shelf.

I was living the entrepreneurial dream I'd imagined … but life had other plans.

## WHEN EVERYTHING CHANGED

I'd been balancing long days as a psychologist, business owner, mother, wife, friend. And … I loved every moment.

As an ADHDer, running had always been my therapy, my rhythm, my way of processing the world. Lunchtime breaks involved going for a 5k run and coming back revitalised, clear-headed, ready to conquer the world.

Over the course of a year, that changed. Running became harder, then impossible. The fatigue had no clear cause and I couldn't shake it. It was frustrating – I was filled with passion, not burnout. Something was wrong, but I couldn't name it … until the day the cancer was big enough to be found.

The diagnosis hit like a punch to the stomach; sudden and disorienting. I remember studying the specialist's face for clues about how scared to be. This wasn't supposed to happen to someone like me, at this stage of life, at this moment in my business journey. I was fit, healthy, building the life I'd dreamed of.

Yet there it was. Cancer doesn't ask permission. It doesn't check your calendar.

I was angry. And I was scared ... terrified that I had only months left to live.

Surgery was scheduled for one week later. I asked for two. Two weeks to decide what mattered most. Fourteen days to sit with my children and memorise their faces, wondering if I'd see them grow up. Fourteen days to face the business decisions that suddenly seemed both critically important and utterly meaningless.

I felt the weight of responsibility for my staff. Their livelihoods depended on me and I couldn't even guarantee I'd be there next year. I couldn't fight cancer and manage multiple business locations simultaneously. The mental load of facing mortality as a wife and mother, made every business challenge I'd ever faced seem trivial.

Something had to give. Every option carried loss. This wasn't a failure of planning; reality had simply changed the game.

The choice was brutal. I closed that newly opened second clinic – the one with the harbour views, the one I'd been standing in dreaming of the future. It felt like amputating a limb. Years of work, investment, all my dreams – cut away.

Sometimes the bravest business decision is knowing what to let go.

## WHAT FRAGILITY TAUGHT ME ABOUT STRENGTH

Cancer stripped me bare. The journey home from hospital was agony – feeling every bump in the road, my husband's hands white-knuckled on the steering wheel, every jolt a reminder of how little control I had, how exposed and fragile I'd become.

I tried hard to wear a brave face. Beside me, my husband wore his. Fear is contagious and we didn't want our children to catch ours.

I'd built my identity around strength. I was the capable one, the problem-solver, the woman who'd emigrated countries, completing a doctorate while having children and building a business. Strength was my currency, my brand, my superpower.

Suddenly, I was terrifyingly fragile.

I couldn't dress myself. Could barely walk from the house to the car. The treatment was relentless; surgery that left both visible and invisible scars, fatigue that showed up to every event, every decision and every moment I tried to push through.

Every time I pushed too hard, cognitive fog would roll in and simple tasks became impossible. I had to learn to respect my new limits, even as I resented them. There were days when my achievement was simply *made it downstairs today.* It was humbling.

I fought the change with everything I had. It was not graceful, or pretty. I was a psychologist; I knew intellectually I needed to rest. Yet here I was, resisting, grieving the loss of the woman who was always producing, always achieving. That version of me was my identity; I did not want to let her go.

But in that resistance, something unexpected was growing.

When you can't chase the next milestone, you notice the warmth of your child's hand in yours. When there is no way out of uncertainty, you become grateful just to see another sunrise. When you stop sweating the small stuff, you discover what actually deserves your energy.

Gratitude became my anchor. Not because I was trying to be positive or spiritual, but because it was the only thing that quieted the fear. Our brains are wired to scan for threats, to focus on what's wrong or missing.

It's a survival mechanism, but it keeps us stuck in anxiety. Each small moment I noticed – the warmth of my child's hand, the sunlight on my face, the fact that I was still here, every tiny moment of gratitude - gave me strength.

It shifted my focus from what I might lose to what I still had. From fear to presence.

Cancer had taken my energy, but it also clarified my values with laser precision. Slowing down forced me to ask different questions:

- What really matters?
- How do I want to spend whatever energy I have?
- What difference do I most want to make?

The answers surprised me. And they would reshape everything about how I built my business moving forward.

## BEGINNING AGAIN, DIFFERENTLY

When I returned to work, I thought I'd be content with *just being alive*. And I did feel deeply grateful. But here's what I learned - survival isn't the same as living. Alongside that gratitude, there was a pull I couldn't ignore … the desire to create again, to build, to reach further. At first, I felt guilty. *Why did I want more when I'd already been given a second chance? Why push when fatigue remained my demanding business partner?* But the entrepreneur in me refused to stay quiet. Purpose, I was learning, is essential - not just for business, but for life.

I couldn't rebuild what I'd had before. Those visions of multiple locations were gone and I grieved them. But in that grief, space opened for something new.

Opportunity arrived unexpectedly; a building became available. Huge. Beautiful. Nothing I'd been looking for, and certainly not something I felt ready for. The rent alone terrified me – I'd need to double the size of our practice to make the numbers work.

Every rational voice in my head screamed *'too risky, too soon, too much.'*

I was not ready. The timing was not perfect. But when opportunities align with your deeper purpose, you have to trust the moment and act.

I signed the lease. Then I did something that would have seemed absurd in my pre-cancer life - I negotiated a break clause if my cancer recurred. Morbidly real. Pragmatically necessary. A reminder that entrepreneurial thinking doesn't stop just because life gets hard – it adapts.

I stepped forward into something I couldn't have imagined before cancer changed everything.

## LESSONS FROM MY JOURNEY
### 1. There Is No Perfect Time

When I signed that lease for the new building, I wasn't thinking about perfect timing. I was thinking about purpose. About the vision that had survived cancer. About the opportunity that was right in front of me, regardless of whether I felt "ready."

You'll never feel fully ready for the things that matter most – and that's okay. Courage isn't the absence of fear; it's the decision to start anyway.

When I opened my first practice, I wasn't ready. I didn't have every system perfected or every risk eliminated. When I expanded after cancer, I didn't know for sure that I'd survive to see it succeed. But I had a vision and a deep willingness to act.

We tell ourselves we'll start when things are calmer, when the kids are older, when we feel more confident, when we have more certainty. But certainty is an illusion, and "later" may never come.

Life is unpredictable. Market shifts, family emergencies, health scares, economic downturns – there will always be another curveball. The businesses that survive aren't the ones with perfect plans, but the ones that can bend without breaking. Entrepreneurs thrive not by avoiding uncertainty, but by learning to dance with it.

The building, the offer, the conversation that feels "too soon" may in fact be the invitation you've been waiting for. Opportunities have expiration dates. Learn to recognise the moments that align with your purpose and take calculated risks.

Start Today: What idea are you perfecting instead of launching? What conversation are you preparing for instead of having? Take one concrete step toward the thing that scares and excites you most. Send the email. Make the call. Say yes to the next right opportunity – even if you don't feel ready yet.

## 2. Redefine Success on Your Own Terms

Before cancer: Success meant growth. More clients, more locations, more milestones. Numbers on a spreadsheet, external validation, visible proof that I was winning. I measured my worth by how much I could scale, how fast I could expand.

After cancer: Success meant something entirely different. It meant waking up to see the faces of my husband and children. It meant doing work that mattered deeply to me, even if it was smaller in scope. It meant sustainable growth that honoured my energy and values rather than burning me out. It meant having the courage to negotiate that break clause – to build a business that could flex with my life, not demand I sacrifice my life for it.

Same business, completely different definition of winning.

Standing in that hospital room, facing mortality, none of those metrics I'd been using to define success mattered. What mattered was time with my children. The quality of my work. The impact I made on the lives I touched. Whether I was building something sustainable or burning myself out chasing someone else's version of success.

True success means showing up as who you really are, pursuing what genuinely lights you up, and being willing to adapt when life throws you curveballs. It's messy, it's real, and it looks different for everyone.

Stop chasing someone else's definition of success. What genuinely excites you? What problems do you love solving? What would success look like if no one else was watching?

**Start Today:** Write your own definition of success. What would have to be true for you to feel genuinely successful, regardless of what others might think?

## 3. Sustainable Leadership Begins With You

As women, we often push ourselves to breaking point. We tell ourselves rest comes later. After the work is done, after everyone else's needs are met.

But later may never come.

Cancer taught me this lesson the hard way. I'd built my identity around being the capable one, the one who could handle it all. Until I couldn't. Until my body forced me to stop.

You face these moments in business too – moments when you must choose between options that all involve loss. In psychology, we call it a struggle choice point. Not a failure of courage or planning, but a moment life changes the rules and forces you to decide what matters most.

For me, it was choosing between my health and rapid business growth. I couldn't have both. I had to close that second location to protect what mattered most: my life, my health, my family. That decision felt like failure at the time. Now I understand it was leadership – clear-eyed, values-driven leadership.

You can't lead with clarity or courage when you're disconnected from your own needs, values, and purpose. Sustainable leadership starts with being true to yourself.

Make time for what sustains you. Move your body. Sleep deeply. Hug your family. Walk in nature. Follow your passions.

And just as importantly – let go of what's not essential. We often hold on too tightly to relationships, systems, or habits that drain rather than fuel us. Authentic leadership comes from aligning your energy and actions with what truly matters to you.

Rest is not a reward for finishing. It's the foundation that lets you keep building.

**Start Today:** Identify one thing in your life or business that you need to stop doing, delegate, or eliminate entirely. What are you holding onto that's draining rather than fuelling you?

## YOUR TIME IS NOW!

The title of this book says it all: Begin It Now.

Are you waiting for the *right time*? When the children are older, when you have more savings, when you feel more confident, more certain?

The perfect time doesn't exist.

Life will interrupt. Challenges don't end your story, they shape it. They reveal your strength, refine your focus and remind you what truly matters.

So begin now. Start small if you must. Take one step toward your dreams. Have the conversation you've been rehearsing. Write the first paragraph. Submit the application. Launch the pilot program.

You don't need to know how your story ends. You just need to begin.

Not tomorrow. Not when it's easier. Not when fear, exhaustion and uncertainty magically disappear.

Your dream – that business idea, that career change, that creative project – deserves to get started.

Begin it now.

# AMANDA MULLIN

Dr. Amanda Mullin is a Clinical Psychologist, keynote speaker, and writer whose life's work is helping people thrive. She is the founder of Mindworx Psychology and Think Differently, multi-award-winning ventures that reflect her commitment to excellence, neurodiversity, and mental wellbeing.

Amanda's journey has been shaped by curiosity and courage: after completing her first psychology degree, she managed a pub, built and sold a business, and travelled the world before retraining in holistic therapies and, later, as a Doctor of Psychology. She emigrated to Australia in her thirties, creating one of the country's leading private practices.

When a breast cancer diagnosis disrupted everything she had built, Amanda learned firsthand that there is no perfect time to begin. Guided by gratitude, compassion, and authenticity, she now teaches and trains businesses, schools, and individuals on mental health, neurodiversity, and emotional regulation.

She lives in Sydney with her husband, children and dog.

# LETTERS TO MY YOUNGER SELF

## ANNA ABESADZE

Dear Reader,

These letters began as quiet confessions - written in the spaces between what was lived and what was understood. They are not declarations, but invitations. Whispers passed from one season of life to another. A flicker of hope held up against the dark. Learning, slowly, that *having a voice* has always mattered.

You'll find no perfect answers here. Just the honest weight of becoming. The trembling certainty is that even in our doubt, there is direction. That softness, too, can stand its ground. And that stories - when shared without shame - can light the path for those still wandering.

These pages are a reminder that growth is not linear, nor is healing quiet. We do not bloom despite our questions, but because of them. And as George Eliot once wrote, *'It is never too late to be what you might have been.'*

So, wherever this chapter finds you, whether at the beginning, an ending, or somewhere achingly in between - may it offer you this simple truth; you don't need permission to begin again. You are already enough. And the becoming has already begun.

With all my heart,

Anna

## LETTER #1: TO THE LITTLE GIRL ON THE BALCONY WHO WONDERS

Dear Anna,

Have you ever struggled to understand how your voice could carry weight in a world that often overlooks where you come from?

You sit on the balcony of your childhood home, mountains rising in the distance like quiet guardians, your thoughts already drifting far beyond what you see. You are so young, barely fourteen, and yet inside you are a storm of questions and dreams. There's a fire in you - an early ambition that doesn't quite have a name yet, only questions:

Why not more?

Why not you?

Why does the world feel both so close and so far away?

And, why does it ache so deeply when your ideas are met not with curiosity, but with ironic smiles or quiet dismissal—as if your voice were too bold, too young, too much?

You don't yet know that this curiosity is a gift - one that will guide you, shape you, and lead you through every uncertain chapter. Remember, you don't need to have it all figured out. Stay curious, kind and rooted.

Let that same curiosity lead you, even when the answers take time to arrive. And when the world doesn't offer you a way forward, don't hesitate to carve your own path. You've done it before - founding the clubs you wished existed, shaping spaces for your school and town. That's not just initiative, it's vision. Keep building what you can't find. That's how change begins. Don't wait for permission or perfection - act anyway.

But curiosity alone is not enough. What truly sets you apart is your kindness; often underestimated, yet quietly transformative. Your softness is not a flaw, but a quiet kind of strength. Guard it well.

# BEGIN IT NOW

This strength first showed itself when you, still in high school, stepped up to voluntarily teach English in your hometown. No one asked you to, and yet you showed up anyway. You gave your time, your energy, your heart. And while some offered doubt instead of support, whispers questioning your worth, you kept going. Despite the noise, you made space where there was none. You created something out of nothing. And most importantly, you changed lives.

Let others mistake tenderness for weakness. Your compassion is your superpower. Quiet confidence speaks louder than noise, and true strength lies in courage, integrity and showing up ... with your whole heart.

Along the way, don't forget to extend that same compassion inward. Be gentle with yourself too, especially on days when doubt creeps in or things don't go as planned. Self-compassion is not a luxury, it's a necessity. Forgive yourself for stumbles and setbacks, as they do not define you, but shape you.

Celebrate every small win because they matter. Those moments of progress, no matter how tiny, build the foundation for bigger change and remind you of your strength.

And when it feels like nothing is moving - be patient. Be patient in slow seasons, they are preparing you. When it's your time, don't shrink. Make space. Lead with heart.

You may never feel ready – but do it anyway. Speak, build, begin - even when your voice shakes. The world needs your true voice.

Begin now.

With love,

Your 33-year-old self.

## LETTER #2: TO THE STUDENT STANDING AT THE AIRPORT

Dear Anna,

You're at the airport; passport in one hand, dreams in the other. This isn't just a boarding pass, it's proof that persistence works. Three applications. Three rounds of hope and heartbreak. And now, you're the first from your hometown to win this exchange program and study in the US for a year. You're not just crossing borders, you're breaking barriers.

I know your heart is racing. You're excited but also scared. You don't know what's waiting on the other side. *Will you fit in? Will you be good enough? Will you make your family and hometown proud?*

Let me tell you something gently, but clearly: *You already have.*

Getting on that plane is not just about where you're going, it's about who you choose to become. A girl who kept showing up. A girl who didn't give up when 'no' came more than once. A girl who dared to believe there was something more, not because she was running from home, but because she loved it enough to carry it with her.

You'll learn quickly that the world is vast, beautiful and complicated. Not everyone will understand your story, your accent or your questions. And that's okay. What matters is that you keep learning, listening and walking forward with humility and strength.

You're not just a student abroad, you're a bridge. You carry your country with you; the flavours, the warmth, the grit, the songs. You represent more than yourself now. But don't let that pressure weigh you down. Let it remind you that you belong in every room you enter.

You will feel lonely sometimes. You will doubt yourself. But in those moments, I want you to remember that this is what courage looks like. It's not loud or perfect. It's quiet, steady and rooted in something deeper than fear.

And from where I stand- at 33 - I can tell you, every challenge will shape you. Every stumble will teach you. Every connection will open a new place in your heart. So don't hold back. Ask the questions. Join the conversation. Let the world change you ... but never let it erase you.

You were meant to go. You were meant to grow. And yes, you were meant to come back stronger.

With so much pride,

Someone who knows the road ahead is bright.

## LETTER #3: TO THE WOMEN AT THE TABLE WHO BUILT BRIDGES WITH ACCENTS

Dear Anna,

You walked into those rooms, bright-eyed and full of purpose, carrying ideas and a will to serve. They tried to make you doubt; too young, too foreign, too softly spoken. You heard it in smirks and dismissals, not just words.

I see you at that long table, youngest by a decade, your notepad full, your heart hopeful. You weren't there to dominate but to serve, to build, to lead quietly with grace and grit. Yet servant leadership is often mistaken for weakness.

Remember the time they mocked your accent … as if it defined your worth. What they didn't know was that you mastered code-switching across five cultures, carrying migration in your bones. Let them laugh. If roles were reversed, would they even try?

When they mock your voice, they reveal their limits, not yours. Respond with clarity, not apology. Prepare twice as hard, speak half as much, and let your work speak loudest. As Eleanor Roosevelt said, *'No one can make you feel inferior without your consent.'* Hold that power.

And to that kind American host grandma, who saw your fire before you did … thank you. She reminded you that kindness and confidence can coexist, and her steady belief in you still echoes in the choices you make today.

You've been burned by envy, doubted for generosity, told kindness is a mask. But you learned to set boundaries with a soft voice and firm ground. You learned hierarchy doesn't command respect – you earn it. You learned to hold space without apology.

You document your wins, not for revenge, but resilience. When doubt storms, your work anchors you.

Yes, some tried to dim your light, calling it *too much*. You cried, you panicked, your body paid the price. But look at you - five countries, witnessing injustice's many faces – still kind, still generous, but sharper. Protect your energy like the rare gift it is.

They call it accent – you call it legacy. Immigration reshaped you, gave you belonging in many places, and most importantly, to yourself.

Leadership isn't loud – it's listening hardest, lifting others, dreaming in rooms where no one looks like you. When you mentor, sit with younger you and remind her; *yes, the world is unfair, but your light won't be dimmed.*

Now, build tables where no one feels small, where every voice speaks before judgment. Systems change … not with titles, but with example. Be that example.

Lead on, Anna. Kindly. Fiercely. Deservedly.

With love,

Someone who's walked this path.

## LETTER #4: TO THE WOMAN BALANCING DIAPERS AND DEADLINES

You're tired. Bone-deep tired. The kind that sleep can't fix. You're juggling lullabies and leadership, diapers and deadlines - and in the middle of it all, you wonder if your dreams still matter. You feel guilty for wanting more … and guilty for not doing enough. But hear this, motherhood didn't pause your mission. It deepened it.

You once imagined that motherhood would mark a slowing down. That you'd sip mint tea in the yard and watch your kids run barefoot

# BEGIN IT NOW

through the grass. But the world didn't soften. It sped up and demanded you evolve, keep learning, keep showing up in rooms that rarely waited for you to catch your breath.

And now, as you consider your PhD, that guilt creeps in. *Can you really take on more?* But this isn't stepping away from your children, it's stepping into a life where they see their mother still daring, still curious, still becoming. You're doing it for the little hands watching you type, think, lead.

You wear both hats with pride … but also with weight. Trying to be everything to everyone, bent your back in ways no one could see.

Here's something to live by – if it's not essential and it costs you presence with your children, it can wait. Make a list of non-negotiables, not for work, but for motherhood; the bedtime talk, the weekend walk, the meal without screens. Anchor your days around those.

Let me tell you something hard but true – you won't regret skipping a meeting. But you'll regret missing Lukas' whispered question or Lily's living room dance. Your job will survive if you take a break, but your children might not forget if you never do.

Rest is not weakness. Boundaries are not disloyalty. Working late might look like dedication – but if it chips away at your health or your joy, it's not sustainable. Not for your students. Not for your dreams.

Burnout is not a badge of honor. Build recovery into your calendar. Block off time for *non-urgent joy*; a bath, a book, a walk. Not earned - just necessary.

You are not falling behind when you pause. You are honoring your energy so you can last.

Let yourself grieve the quiet you imagined. Feel the anger at the unfairness. Rest without guilt.

And please, never forget; motherhood didn't weaken you. It expanded you. Your voice is stronger. Your purpose deeper. You're not just building a career, you're building a legacy. Your children and your students are watching a woman who dares to keep going, not because she never tires, but because she knows when to stop, breathe and begin again.

So, here's my advice:

Protect your peace like it's part of your job – because it is. Say no, even if your voice trembles. Let the dishes wait. Let someone else lead the meeting. Go sit in that yard. Watch your children laugh in the grass. That is what they'll remember. And maybe, just maybe, that's what will keep you going too.

With fierce love and deep pride,
Your Future Self.

These letters are a quiet archive of the roads walked - from the little girl on the balcony asking *Why not me?* to the young woman at the airport holding both dreams and doubt, to the mother balancing lullabies and leadership, and the leader who kept showing up with ideas, kindness, and a quiet fire that wouldn't go out. These pages are stitched together by your voice; a voice that never waited for permission, even when it shook.

You thought softness was weakness, until you learned it was your power. You thought you had to choose between being a mother and being ambitious, until you realised motherhood didn't pause your mission, it deepened it. You believed you needed to do more, be more, know more. But all along, the only thing you needed was to trust this truth; *you already are enough – and you already began.*

And to you, dear reader – stranger, yet somehow close – if you've ever felt too small, too late, too uncertain to matter, let this book whisper otherwise. You do not have to be ready. You do not have to be perfect. You only have to begin.

Let these letters be your permission slip. To dream again. To rest without guilt. To speak even if your voice trembles. To lead with heart.

# BEGIN IT NOW

To start before you're sure.

When everything feels too much – too loud, too late, too heavy – pause and ask yourself:

What hurts right now?

What do I need to feel safe with it?

What have I been pretending is fine?

And what would happen if I stopped pretending?

What would help me feel like I belong - to myself, to this moment, to something true?

Then take one small, honest step toward that belonging. That's how you begin again. That's how you come back to yourself.

Because no matter your chapter, no matter the weight you carry, the right time isn't someday – it's now.

So, turn the page, take the step, write the story that only you can.

As Arthur Ashe wisely put it: *'Start where you are. Use what you have. Do what you can.*

Begin it now!

With all my heart,

Anna

… a stranger who sees you, and believes you already began.

# ANNA ABESADZE

Anna Abesadze is an award-winning advisor and educator with extensive experience across North America, Europe, and Asia. She currently serves as Adviser to the Rector and Lecturer at Grigol Robakidze University, leading strategic initiatives, international collaborations, and educational innovation. Additionally, Anna serves as Global Governance Coordinator at World Vision International, where she supports governance on a global scale.

Anna is dedicated to advancing education, youth development, and women's leadership. Her impactful work has been recognized internationally, including honors such as the Woman Changing the World Awards' Leader of the Year (2024), GISR Foundation's Woman Changemaker of the Year (2024), and finalist for the GESS Award for Outstanding Contributions in Education (2023). She also holds the President's Volunteer Service Award from the White House and the Host Country Hero Award from Peace Corps Georgia.

Anna co-authored *Women Living Fearlessly* (New York) and *Authenticity and Action* (London), focusing on leadership, empowerment, and change. In 2025, she is embarking on her PhD journey in the fields of international partnerships and management, furthering her research and impact.

Anna is also a proud mother to Lukas and Lily, to whom she dedicates this chapter, with love and hope for their bright futures.

# STEEL CAPS, STILETTOS & STUFF THEY SAID I COULDN'T DO

### GINA FIELD

I'll never forget the day I told Mum I'd applied to be a security officer.

She was in the kitchen - where she always sat, running the household like a mafia boss -and without missing a beat, she screamed out, "You can't even sleep with the light off, and you wanna work night shift?" *Groan.*

Fair call, Mum. But I was 19. And 19-year-olds are a perfect mix of invincible and completely delusional. It was 1988 - big hair, bigger shoulder pads, no mobile phones and even bigger opinions about what women shouldn't do.

At the time, I was working at a local hardware store, surrounded by men who assumed I didn't know what a bolt cutter was unless it came in pink. Then came this guy - every day, same time, same crisp uniform. He had a presence. He had a security job. I wanted that -I loved the uniform and the feeling of authority.

One day I asked him, 'How do I get a security job like yours?' And with an instant reply he said, 'You don't. It's not a job for a woman,' … with almost a sarcastic laugh and a couple of eye rolls.

Now, here's the kicker … he wasn't wrong. I mean, looking back,

# GINA FIELD

I don't think I'd ever seen a female security officer or a female police officer, at that time. It just wasn't a thing. If you were a woman, your career choices basically boiled down to nurse, receptionist or homemaker - something more traditional (So to speak). Mum would always say to me 'Why do you always have to prove a point Gina?' I would just shrug my shoulders and say, 'I dunno Mum, it's something I wanna do.' And then go hang upside down on the poor bent wash line out the back.

But something switched in me. That quiet, defiant little voice in the back of my mind whispered; 'Watch me.' Along with a mantra that has stayed with me for … nearly forever 'Never say never. What's the worst that could happen? They say no.'

It's funny looking back now, decades later, running one of the most awarded security companies in Australia. Because honestly? I didn't even know what I was signing up for back then. All I knew, was that I wasn't going to be told *I couldn't do something* simply because I was born a woman … my only crime at the time.

So I did it. I applied. Got the job. Bought the boots. I still slept with the hallway light on - I just did it after a 12-hour night shift. Back then, women were expected to stay behind a desk - because apparently - we weren't 'coordinated enough' to do anything else.

Every school report card basically said the same thing: 'Talks too much. Distracts others.' Report card day was like a full-blown military operation in my house. I'd come running through the door, hide the envelope somewhere creative - behind the toaster, under the couch, once in the dog's kennel, praying my dog would eat it - then bolt straight out the back to play, thinking maybe, just maybe, they'd forget it existed.

Cue Dad. Glasses sliding down the end of his nose, shirt off, work pants unbuttoned, stomach hanging proudly over his belt. It wasn't a great look, trust me on that. 'Do you wanna explain this to me, Gina?'

And of course, the funny, colourful Gina took over … and they could barely keep a straight face.

The truth is, both my parents were incredibly hard workers. My dad was a butcher, my mum a nurse - and both of them held second jobs just to keep food on the table. I come from extremely humble, low-income beginnings. There was nothing fancy about our life but there was a lot of heart, grit, and *get-it-done* energy. That foundation shaped everything I am today.

They both knew that high school didn't click for me. I wasn't stupid, far from it - I was sharp, quick-witted and could talk my way out of a crime scene. I had a big personality, but I struggled to sit still, stay focused, and do what the system told me. I would climb trees and jump the closed gates. I sometimes wonder if I had a listening or learning disorder - or maybe just a low tolerance for boredom and BS. Either way, I knew the traditional work path wasn't for me.

This is the part that really confuses people; I actually love discipline. Structure. Routine. A crisp, neat school uniform with the socks pulled up just right. I was a walking contradiction (which, might I add, I'm still known for today). I was a total tomboy ... but I loved pink. Go figure.

I'd collect the lunches for the class, carry the roll call folder like it was the crown jewels, and practically fight people to be the one making announcements. I was the loudest kid in the room, but somehow, also the most reliable when it came to anything that looked official. I was never sick and always early for school.

Naturally, they made me a prefect. Not for academic brilliance ... let's not kid ourselves ... but because I was popular, organised (many saying I had almost obsessive-compulsive attributes), and had a voice that could carry across an oval. Almost like an *accidental leader...* and honestly, that title has stuck ever since.

So, in 1988, I got a security job. That moment alone was a story and a half; especially with three blokes practically heckling me through the interview process. I was too young and naïve at the time to realise it.

The uniform? Issued. And of course, it was a men's cut, no woman's back then - so tight it nearly sliced me in half. Roster? Set. And me? Standing there with this wild mix of nerves, pride, and a sense of – *'I bloody did it.'*

As Queen once sang: *Don't stop me now.*

I am led to believe I was one of very few women in the entire security industry back then. Emphasis on few. I wasn't just the odd one out - I was the only one out.

The backlash was immediate. My first boss, bless him, (rest his soul) had a female on his team (what did he do wrong to cop that). He was like something out of a sitcom. He looked like Danny DeVito; full-blown Short Man Syndrome. Swore like it was a second language. And I vividly remember, he used to spit when he spoke.

It's funny, isn't it? The people who shape us - good, bad and feral - are always the ones we remember most.

Back in those days, there was no such thing as Human Resources. No bullying claims. No mentors. You just copped it on the chin and kept going. *Suck it up*, as they say … and that I did.

Yet, to this day, I thank him. He didn't break me; he built me. One explosive tantrum at a time.

Then came the big test. I was sent to a construction site. A proper, full-on, rebar-and-hi-vis kind of site. And guess what? I was the only woman there. Again, my job was to sit at the front gate.

Even better - I had to share the porta-loos. Let me tell you, nothing will humble you faster than opening a plastic toilet door after a bunch of sweaty tradies have had their morning bacon rolls. Let's just say it was a safety risk in itself. Speaking of safety risks – apparently … I was one!

The union bosses decided I wouldn't be able to 'protect' the site if something went wrong.

# BEGIN IT NOW

And that was it. No warning. No performance issue. Just – *'You're a woman. You can't do this.'*

And I lost my job. Just like that - *simply because of the sex I was born.*

But I didn't retreat; I recalibrated. I've always said – *'what doesn't kill you will just make you stronger - it makes you sharper, louder, and absolutely unstoppable.'*

So, I asked my boss if I could become a mobile patrol officer. This is a job role where you drive around all night and check different sites.

His response?

'Hell NO. Are you mentally deranged?' I took that as a No ... I guess.

I was 20. All of 5'4" and full of fire. 'Women can't do that job. Get back to the desk. You're good for answering phones.'

So, behind his back, I started going out with the boys on patrols ... in my own time. I learned the runs. I learned everything.

Then came a Friday night.

No mobile drivers. All off sick. He was desperate - throwing staplers, paper flying everywhere, yelling so hard I thought the walls would crack. That ... and spit. Lots of it. His face was so red I honestly thought his head was going to explode.

I came clean. 'I know the runs. I've been doing them,' I told him.

He stared at me. I could see the cogs turning in his mind: A woman... in the mobile patrol division? But he was desperate. 'Right. First, you're getting a written warning. Second, grab the car keys. Third, grab a gun - but don't load it. I don't want you shooting anyone tonight.'

Now, I'd never handled a six-shooter before. Honestly, that terrified me more than the new job itself. But I ran out of that office like I'd just won Lotto; completely snookered him but grinning ear to ear. And like that - I was on the road. Doing the runs, just like the boys. And I reckon a few of them quietly loved it too.

I'm led to believe that made me one of the first female mobile patrol officers in NSW.

And I was bloody good at it.

After years of having my promotion applications shredded. A few years later, I was offered a role as Area Manager. I was elated.

'It's a crap area, crap run ... and it's losing money,' the boss said.

'I'll take it,' I said, without a second thought. *I can do this.*

The area was Penrith NSW Australia. Over the years, I built it up, tripled the run, knew the clients, and knew their dogs' names. I worked literally day and night – seven days a week- no break.

And then, eight days before Christmas, 1997 - they pulled the rug out. Made redundant. The company decided they wanted the run back *in-house* ... now that it was profitable. A new boss had taken over. No thanks. No warning. No loyalty.

And the part that really stung? That company was meant to be my retirement plan; I loved it with all my heart.

So, at the age of 30, I had no money, a car that needed clutch-starting, a flea-bitten dog with a bung leg, no rent, no plan ... and zero idea what I was going to do.

To say goodbye to my clients, I handwrote Christmas cards to each and every one of them, and slipped them under their doors. *Thank you and goodbye. I won't be back next year.* I signed them simply, *Gina xx* I did include my phone number, but it was purely a good bye and Thank you.

In 1998, Helen Andrews from Rex Andrews Transport rang me. She'd received my Christmas card. 'Why don't you start your own security company? I'll be your first client.' Helen, now in her 80s and still working, has no idea how famous she is. She's in all of my talks. We all need a *Helen*, don't we? 'Okay, let's do this!' I squealed.

Since then, I've taken home more than 35 industry awards - including the NSW Premier's Businesswoman of the Year and the global *Women Changing the World Award,* up against women from 55 countries.

# BEGIN IT NOW

I've grown my company to nearly 50 staff, secured major government contracts, and built a turnover of seven million dollars. These days, I'm regularly called on by national media - TV, radio, newspapers, you name it - as a trusted voice in the security space. And yes, I've written a book. This one, in fact - alongside so many other incredible women featured in these pages.

Not bad for someone who started as *just a minion* with no formal business training, financial backing or money. That's why I call myself *the accidental leader*, the business misfit who didn't fit the mould … and didn't need to.

And here's the kicker; even now, there are still fewer than a handful of women in Australia who wholly and solely own and operate a physical and electronic security company. So yeah - I'm still standing. And I'm still proving them wrong.

My leadership style has always been simple; lead by example, treat people how you'd want to be treated, lace up your boots, and work shoulder to shoulder with your team. I've never bought into the myth that bigger means better. I've watched too many businesses chase shiny new offices and massive overheads, only to lose sight of what actually matters. Customers don't care about your ego, car or your office space … they care about service. Real service. Quality over quantity. That's what I've always lived by - and it's worked. If your team respects you, they'll jump out of the trenches for you and give you 110% every time.

One of the things I'm most proud of these days is hearing from women, through emails, messages, and conversations, telling me that I've inspired them to step into diverse industries or take the leap into their own startup. Whether it's through my community mentoring with young women or simply sharing my story like this book, I somehow became an accidental advocate for the physical security industry. It wasn't something I set out to do, but here I am, known as a trailblazer in a space where women were once almost invisible.

If I've learned anything, it's this: *you don't need to wait for permission, blow your own trumpet - no one is going to do it for you.*

And don't let anyone tell you that you can't. Because that's exactly when you must look them dead in the eye and say; 'Watch me. Never say never. What's the worst that could happen? They say No.'

So … begin it now. Even if you're terrified. Even if you've got no plan. It doesn't matter. What matters most is that you start. Your way!

# GINA FIELD

Gina Field is the founder and Managing Director of Nepean Regional Security, one of Australia's most awarded and recognised security companies, based in Sydney, New South Wales. What began as a humble kitchen bench startup in 1998 has grown into a multimillion-dollar business with nearly 50 staff, a fleet of patrol vehicles, and a portfolio that includes major government contracts, iconic venues, and high-profile clients.

Raised in a hard-working, blue-collar household, Gina's roots are in resilience. Her father was a butcher, her mother a nurse—both working multiple jobs to make ends meet. With no silver spoon or fancy business degree, Gina turned sheer determination, grit, and a lot of heart into a business empire.

She entered the security industry in the late 1980s—a time when women were barely seen, let alone heard, in the field. Told point-blank she couldn't do the job because she was a woman, Gina defied the odds and proved every doubter wrong. She became, by all accounts, one of the first female mobile patrol officers in New South Wales. She later stepped into a management role, before being made redundant just eight days before Christmas. Instead of giving up, she regrouped, and with a phone

# GINA FIELD

call from a supportive client, launched her own company.

That leap of faith became a legacy.

Today, Gina is not only a business owner but also a trailblazer, keynote speaker on women in leadership, and a fierce advocate for diversity in male-dominated industries. She has won over 35 prestigious business and industry awards, including the NSW Premier's Businesswoman of the Year and the *Women Changing the World Award* against competitors from 55 countries.

Known for her mix of high heels and high standards, Gina is what she calls a "walking contradiction"—tough as nails but loves pink, glam, and sparkle. She's worked in Kings Cross, pubs, clubs, secured movie sets, and rubbed shoulders with celebrities—while also helping rewrite the rules of what leadership in security looks like.

A recognised security expert, Gina is a regular media contributor across national TV, radio, and newspapers. She's been featured on *Sunrise*, *2GB*, *2CC*, *3AW*, and beyond, often speaking on issues from public safety to industry reform. She's also the long-running columnist behind "Left of Field," a popular tongue-in-cheek column that captures her humorous take on human behaviour and frontline experiences.

From working-class beginnings to running a 24/7 security operation, Gina's story is one of resilience, leadership, and unapologetic authenticity. She proves you don't need permission, a perfect plan, or a powerful title to lead—you just need to begin it now.

Website: nepeanregionalsecurity.com.au
ginafield.com.au

# TO LIVE FULLY IN EACH MOMENT

## JESSICA HANSEN

"Turi kumwe," whispered the gentle Rwandan hero, comforting me in the back of the darkened theatre behind rows of dignitaries and Hollywood stars. "Tuko pamoja," I replied in Swahili. *We are together.*

Three months prior, I was a world away. Back home in small town Oklahoma after graduate school, scrolling through job listings online, trying in vain to determine how to put my new master's degree in International Development to meaningful use ... and wondering why anyone, particularly an esteemed institution like the United Nations, might consider hiring a small town nobody like me.

That night, I saw the movie *Hotel Rwanda* for the first time. It left me curled up, sobbing on my parents' couch. I remembered vividly the brutal genocide unfolding on the news a decade earlier, as the world looked on in horror or completely turned away. The film presents the account of Paul Rusesabagina, a hotelier who sheltered over a thousand people throughout the genocide. His story embodies Professor Joseph Campbell's 'hero's journey,' beginning with a moment of need that calls to the hero's soul – one they often wish to refuse but are compelled to rise to the occasion and answer.

The next morning, inspired by Paul's bravery, I decided to heed my own calling. The question *Why a nobody like me?* became *Why not somebody like me?* Setting aside fear and doubt to answer what called to me, I applied for a role with the United Nations High Commissioner for Refugees - the organisation that assisted Rwandan genocide survivors. In three short months, I interviewed for, was offered, and accepted the role. I packed my bags and moved to Washington, DC, where my first assignment was coordinating a World Refugee Day event, honoring none other than Paul Rusesabagina.

What a surreal gift to be the first person to greet him on his 50th birthday, then escort him to Grosvenor Auditorium to introduce a screening of *Hotel Rwanda* where we were met by then-Secretary of State, Condoleezza Rice and Goodwill Ambassador, Angelina Jolie. Having seen the film more times than he could count, in addition to living it first, Paul asked if he could go back and rest during the screening, promising to be back in time for the 'Q&A.' I leaned against the back wall of the theatre and watched it for a second time.

Toward the end of the film, moved to tears yet again, I felt a gentle, comforting squeeze in the dark and looked up to see Paul's kind smile. I'd gone from sobbing on a couch to standing alongside a hero in a matter of months - unknowingly setting my lifelong career into motion - all because I'd dared to answer the call.

## OWN YOUR STORY

Years later, at a high point in that career, I unexpectedly suffered a seizure, then fell unconscious on a flight from Marrakech to Rome. All my muscles, including those controlling my bladder, released completely. A dear friend and colleague carried me off the plane, his jacket wrapped around my waist hiding the wetness of my skirt. Ashamed and mortified, I asked that we never speak of it and pretend everything was fine.

This was actually my second seizure in recent years. Clearly, everything wasn't fine. Depression and anxiety had been knocking loudly but had been ignored for so long, they'd resorted to more extreme measures. Fear of future seizures finally outweighed my shame and I sought professional help. My doctor recommended an MRI, after which the neurologist called exclaiming, "Your brain is perfect!" and "You need a therapist." I was diagnosed with Post Traumatic Stress Disorder (PTSD).

This made sense. I'd chosen a career in humanitarian aid, regularly placing myself in the midst of danger and great human suffering. With therapy, I surprisingly learned that the seizures were caused by something much deeper than my work. I carried scars from violence and pain experienced as a child - experiences that taught me that I was unworthy of love, that told me to suppress my own needs and instead please others for acceptance and survival. Ultimately, that had led me to conclude that I could risk sacrificing myself for the well-being of others because I would never be 'enough.' I was disposable and wouldn't be missed.

Therapy offered gentle inquiry into these long-held beliefs. When and how did they originate? Were they true? Did it serve me to carry them? Was there another way to live? A few weeks later, on a roadtrip with trusted friends, risking rejection and humiliation, I decided to own my story, so that it no longer felt like it owned me. I told them what happened on the plane.

Not only was I met with love, support, and encouragement … but they also offered thanks. The vulnerability and openness around what had previously brought me shame gave others the courage to share parts of themselves they'd long kept hidden too. We allowed ourselves to be fully seen, known, and held by one another, and it's become a regular practice and litmus test for friendship. There's no greater gift we can give - to ourselves and others - than to offer our full selves vulnerably, to meet one another without judgement, and to embrace each other (and ourselves) with unconditional love and acceptance.

# JESSICA HANSEN

## RELEASE THE KNOTS

Until my late twenties, I was terrified of ordering pizza. By the time I could comfortably do so, I'd long since survived war zones and the aftermath of genocide.

My mother immigrated to the US from Thailand after meeting and marrying my father during the Vietnam War. While she impressively speaks many languages, all but Thai carry an accent. As children, my sister and I were oblivious to the underlying racism, stress, and humiliation our mother often endured with whichever impatient, unsympathetic sixteen-year-old answered the line at the neighborhood pizza joint in Oklahoma. She naturally became anxious about this seemingly simple task - a fear we regularly observed and unwittingly inherited - and it went well beyond pizza. We were scared to return VHS tapes to the drop-off chute and terrified to approach checkout counters, certain we were doing everything wrong … all the time. We watched with wonder as others seemed to navigate these nerve-wracking tasks with ease.

Experiencing racism in the States was hardly the only suffering she endured – being pulled out of school in Thailand while her four younger brothers were allowed to continue, having friends tricked into human trafficking, and later managing connection with parts of her Thai family, who refused to accept her 'half-breed' children. My father suffered his own traumas, growing up on a farm in rural America, navigating unhealthy and outdated expectations of masculinity, all before being inadvertently shipped off to a tragic and devastating war. As shown in recent studies on epigenetics - the way behaviours and environment can affect how our genes function - traces of trauma experienced as far back as four generations can still be expressed through our genes today.

My parents never received the space or support they needed to heal. Without meaning to, they passed their wounds along, all while I was accumulating my own. This suffering manifested in me as chronic pain, depression, and eventually, my seizures. The wounds and stories I bore had become deeply buried, disguised as tight, painful knots within my muscles that would require patient attention to release.

These wounds had their purpose. Suppressing my needs and quirks into silence, kept me safe throughout childhood. People-pleasing elicited attention and affection from others, allowing me glimpses of what acceptance, belonging, and love might feel like. Workaholism and martyrdom won me trophies, titles, praise, raises, admiration, and - at least momentarily - a sense of worthiness. The belief that I'd never be *good enough* or deserving of love softened every rejection into an expectation and confirmation of my unworthiness, rather than disappointment.

Some religious practices believe that life's lessons are laid upon our hearts, waiting for them to break, then enter through the cracks to help us heal and grow. Reflecting on these long-held beliefs and behaviours, I can see how they helped the little girl I was to survive and navigate life and its challenges. But they've served their purpose; my heart has grown from the lessons they carried. The woman I am today can thank and release them, moving forward lighter and unburdened. At last, I can order pizzas with fearless ease, while sending love, light, and healing back to my sweet mom.

## FOLLOW YOUR BLISS

My twenties and thirties were spent building what the world called 'success.' I climbed the ladder of my career, each rung offering a better title, salary, and office. I built a picture-perfect life in DC with a kind, successful boyfriend in a cute apartment with an adorable dog and cat. I'd checked the boxes and, by all accounts, looked like I had a relatively perfect life. Still, I couldn't shake the nagging sensation that it felt *all wrong*. It was like I was walking through the world in a gorgeous but ill-fitting suit.

# JESSICA HANSEN

A moment of reckoning arose when I was offered a coveted Director role with the United Nations, with its excellent benefits and prestige. At the same time, an old friend shared an unpaid volunteer opening with a relatively unknown organization in rural Kenya; launching a new initiative to assist communities in creating and scaling their own long-term pathways out of extreme poverty. This project was much more aligned with what I'd found to be the most effective approach to this work, where local populations have full agency and support in creating the change *they* want to see.

Volunteers lived at the same standards as the population with which they were based - no fancy living quarters or amenities. The current team posted photos of venomous spiders, mischievous baboons sabotaging the water supply, and endless accounts of slogging through muddy roads to work with local farmers and teachers. Their photos also contained beautiful rolling green hills with bright blue skies overhead, local schoolhouses brimming with beaming children, and the warm smiles of local community members. The project and photos lit up something inside me that had long gone dim, as I'd tried to build someone else's idea of success. Once again, I felt something calling to my soul. To answer would mean doing the hard but more aligned thing – letting go of the safety of the familiar, rejecting what the world prescribed as fulfillment, and following my *inner knowing* and guidance.

I soon found myself on a bumpy, nine-hour ramshackle bus ride out of Nairobi, with as many squawking chickens as humans aboard. In the rearview I saw my long-term relationship, the fancy apartment and job … and the so-called 'dream life.' They all faded quickly out of view.

What followed included some of the most challenging moments of my life - from hosting colonies of parasites in my intestines to witnessing brutality and loss up-close, to facing recurrent threats from countless creatures and machete-bearing men. It also led to some of the most meaningful work and experiences of my life, fostered some of my deepest friendships, and pushed me to grow stronger and more resilient in all directions. It introduced me to raw and beautiful parts of the world, humanity, and myself. It led me to where I am today ... and there's nowhere I'd rather be.

While some family and friends still don't understand that decision, it was the answer to a calling only I could hear - one from within - where I, *not the external world,* defined purpose and success. Following my inner calling guided me to a fuller, richer, more aligned life; the less fancy 'suit' perfectly tailored just for me. Joseph Campbell advised, 'If you do follow your bliss, you put yourself on a kind of track that has been there all the while, waiting for you, and the life that you ought to be living is the one you are living.'

Follow your bliss and don't be afraid.

## BE CURIOUS

After Kenya, I relocated to San Francisco. Dating apps hadn't existed when I was last stateside but were commonplace when I returned. My first date was with a self-described 'Burner.' I soon learned that this didn't necessarily equate with an unhealthy affinity for fire, but meant he attended an annual event in a Nevada desert where people like him go to 'party.' The guy was a little unusual, so I left the date certain of two things; there would be no second date, and I wasn't interested in this desert-party called Burning Man.

Over the next two years, I noticed that Burning Man was a relatively common and polarising topic in San Francisco. A pattern began to emerge with people falling into two predominant camps. The first seemed to hold judgment about the event and its attendees, even though they'd never been, and weren't open to learning more or going themselves. The other camp, whether they'd been to it or not, seemed lighter and more open about it, generally more curious, adventurous and free.

Walt Whitman suggested we, "be curious, not judgmental." So, I got curious and found myself on another long, bumpy (but this time chickenless) bus ride – this one to the Nevada desert. What I encountered there *was* a 'party' … and it wasn't. In fact, it offered just about anything you could seek. Above all, what I found in greatest abundance was kindness, connection, awe and wonder.

As I took in incredible, towering works of art and danced with abandon with a group of friends, one of them looked over at a group of women, dressed in sparkles, and let out a few snarky judgments about their looks. His judgment hit our ears like a brick wall and felt so out of place … which he instantly realized. It became clear that it said more about how he was doing, *or hurting*, and wasn't about the women at all. *What wound or insecurity would pull him away from the wonder of this place and moment, to focus on something so inconsequential and unkind?* What was the point of belittling anyone, especially over such trivialities? What did it matter what anyone wore, did or said, so long as it brought them joy and didn't harm anyone? I began to realise judgment wasn't just out of place here … it had no place anywhere.

Anytime judgement arises now, I've gotten better at examining it with gentle curiosity and compassion. I look for what *inside me* needs some attention and care. Similar to releasing wounds and knots, releasing judgment brings with it such freedom and ease, healing and growth. The spiritual leader Thich Nhat Hanh encourages us, 'to live fully in each moment and to look on all beings with eyes of compassion.' In practice, I find this guidance can quell any judgment that emerges, especially self-judgment.

To this day, Burning Man remains the single most transformative and life-changing adventure I've undertaken, and I've returned for a decade. It was there, witnessing people of all shapes, sizes, colours and creeds being warmly accepted just as they are, that I was able to accept myself fully, *just as I am*. It's where I experienced real, unconditional love from and for myself for the first time. Where I began to live and believe the most important truth anyone can realise; *there is nothing wrong with me*. There never was and never will be. I'm perfect just as I am, while ever-evolving. My value is and always has been untouchably within me - innate, unchanging and unrelated to my productivity, performance or achievements. I am, always have been, and always will be, worthy and deserving of unconditional acceptance and love. Just like all beings. *Just like you.*

## BEGIN IT NOW

Driving around the stunning New Zealand hills on vacation last year, every roadwork site had a neon orange sign that read: TEMPORARY. What sage wisdom from a construction sign! A replica now hangs above a mirror in our home, an unexpected souvenir reminding us - it's all temporary; we are temporary. Be present. Be kind. As the spiritual guru Ram Dass said, 'We're all just walking each other home.'

Living each moment fully, from that place of deep knowing that all life – your life – is temporary, fleeting, and thus infinitely precious, means that *now is the time* to answer that which calls to your soul, to own the fullness of your story and humanity, to heal old wounds, to release unhelpful triggers and judgement, to be curious, to follow your bliss.

That sounds like a lot to add to what is likely already a long to-do list of things you'd like to achieve - but rest easy. It's not about doing more, it's about doing less and *living more*. Being fully here right now. Deepening your connection with and understanding of yourself, those around you, and the world you live in. Truly experiencing it all. Aligning your life and choices with what calls to your soul, what lights you up. Why wait another moment? The time is now.

## JESSICA HANSEN

According to Bronnie Ware's *Top Five Regrets of the Dying*, the greatest regret is that people wish they'd had the courage to live a life more true to themselves, not the life others expected of them. None of us know how much time we have. You are already enough, sweet friend, you always were. You're ready. Whatever magic you are here to create – *the time to begin is now.*

# JESSICA HANSEN

For over 20 years, Jessica has worked in humanitarian aid, innovation, and social impact, specializing in protection, education, and microfinance. She also loves helping others – from students to adults to nonprofits to corporations – ignite their own capacity to create change. She strives "to live each moment fully, look on all beings with eyes of compassion", and create more safety, peace, and opportunity for all. She's beautifully flawed, ever-evolving, and doing her best to heal, learn, and grow.

Jessica's currently CEO of Alliance for Smiles, an international medical nonprofit that provides free, life-changing surgeries to thousands of children in need across Africa, Asia, and Central and South America, while training and equipping local medical teams to sustainably provide care. She's VP of the Board of WAVO (supporting and educating youth in Ghana), on the board of Mystopia (creating safe spaces for the LGBTQIA+ community), and host of *The HumanKind Podcast*. Jessica is a TEDx speaker and won gold in Human Rights at the 2025 *Women Changing the World Awards & Summit* in London.

Inspired by her Thai mother, Jessica's master's thesis and early work focused on ending human trafficking in Southeast Asia. She

# JESSICA HANSEN

then supported health and human rights programs for Medecins Sans Frontieres and interned at The Centre for Refugee Research to help end rape in refugee camps. This led to her work preventing gender-based violence, ensuring access to rights and opportunity, and shining light on the underserved with many organizations, including the United Nations High Commissioner for Refugees, the International Rescue Committee/Women's Refugee Commission, and the US Committee for Refugees and Immigrants - where she resettled over 11,000 Burundian refugees displaced by genocide.

At Mercy Corps, she engaged youth in global education and change-making, and helped design *The Action Center to End World Hunger* in NYC. Later, she moved to rural Kenya with Nuru International to help communities create their own sustainable pathways out of poverty. At Kiva, she created and led the microfinance and education program *Kiva U* (featured in Chelsea Clinton's book *It's Your World: Get Informed, Get Inspired & Get Going!*), winning the 2013 global Katerva Behavioral Change Award.

She served as Senior Strategist for the Impact Travel Alliance, making travel and tourism more ethical and sustainable, and briefly left the nonprofit world to help tech companies learn to utilize their platforms, products, and people for "good", winning the first-ever Bessie Award in Inclusion in 2019 for her work at Lyft (featured in Oprah's *O Magazine* and over 150 other publications). She helped create the *WePledge 1%* program for Twilio.org, now used by over 40 corporations (including Zoom and Okta) to engage their employees in doing good.

Jessica hopes to always devote her life to helping create a better, safer, healthier world, by inspiring and engaging others to safeguard all that's good while working to positively reshape the rest. She lives in San Francisco, California with her wonderful partner Keven, his two amazing children: Milo and Ollie, and their cats: Ruthie Bader Ginsburg and Maya Angelou.

# THE POWER OF THE FIRST STEP

## LAURA MUIRHEAD

Beginnings are exciting.

Whether it's a new project, a new business or a new trip, there's a natural excitement in starting something new.

New beginnings at times can bring a sense of anxiousness, or even a certain level of fear ... I've had enough beginnings in my life to know all these feelings.

My first dive into entrepreneurship was a bread store. It seemed like such a great idea, modelled after a *supposedly successful* already existing store. The excitement for the potential felt so real! I had a strong desire to step into this world; the world of owning my own business, the world of retail, the world of partnership. I wasn't doing it alone; I brought in my best friend and her husband in as well. Each partner brought their own skills to the table for a seemingly winning combination.

There was so much to learn. I had never leased a commercial space or done a 'build-out' of that space. So many *firsts* came with that project. Hiring an accountant, an attorney, bank loans and meetings in a Chicago high-rise with the high-powered owner of a leasing company. *Who was I to be there?* It felt like such a 'grown-up' world.

The desire to create my own business carried me through. Step by step, I was learning what had to be done. Of course, I wanted to have a successful business. But there were hard lessons learned and in the end … that business closed.

One of the biggest lessons was about believing in people to be truthful. As it turned out, the owner of the business we modelled, our mentor, wasn't honest about his finances. There were other lessons learned along the way. Still, I never questioned my drive to follow through on what I felt called to create. There was no way I wasn't going to begin it when I did.

I didn't expect the next beginning to involve horses, but sometimes, life leads you somewhere you didn't plan to go and it turns out to be exactly where you're meantto be.Again, I had a passion, this time driven by a personal need, to own a horse stable. But because of my previous unsuccessful bread store, I actually argued with myself over starting another business.

I was still feeling the sting of what didn't work the first time around. All the questions were there:

*What if I fail again?*

*What if this is another expensive mistake?*

But underneath the doubt, there was something stronger; a vision I couldn't ignore.

I had been taking riding lessons. It was a passion from childhood that I was finally able to revisit as an adult. Soon enough, I bought a horse. Then the seed of desire to *show horses* was planted. After a thorough search, I found a show horse that would be a good fit for me. I just *knew it* when I rode her the first time.

I was now boarding two horses and working with a trainer. The stable wasn't ideal but it was close to home. Still, it worked … until it didn't. One day, when the stable owner was away, her dog bit my young son. She was unwilling to comply with animal control's requirement to contain the dog after the bite. I knew I couldn't continue at that stable.

Sometimes, the new beginning is created from a need. I needed to move myself and my horses out of that environment.

There was another stable that I tried, but it was just far enough away to make it a challenge with daily life and motherhood. Add to that, one of my horses required medicine twice a day during that time, and it just wasn't practical to continue at that facility.

The search began for a stable to buy. I searched the area with the help of my realtor, even offering to buy the original stable I had boarded at. *Yes, the woman with the dog.* That didn't work out.

Still driven by my desire … I wasn't giving up. A casual conversation with a friend led me to a cornfield that was for sale. *Building a stable* hadn't crossed my mind … until then.

That was exciting. The idea of creating a building that would be exactly what I wanted for my horses. It would be new, thoughtfully designed, and have space for my trainer to offer riding lessons as well. I could picture it so clearly.

But it wasn't just about horses. It was about proving to myself that one failure didn't define me. That I could dream again, build again … and this time, do it on my own terms. So even with the doubts still whispering in the background, I began. Again.

It was another business – another round of lessons to learn. This time, I had to learn about construction, excavation, building fences, timelines, materials and all the unexpected surprises that come with building something from the ground up. Once again, I had to learn who to trust. I hired a contractor who, as it turned out, was taking advantage of the situation and being dishonest. That was tough.

But there were bright spots too. People who stepped in with genuine support. Friends who showed up, helped out and stayed. I'm still close with some of them today.

Looking back, I can see how each beginning built on the one before, even when they didn't seem connected at all. And just when I thought I had it all figured out, life invited me to begin again, in a completely different way.

When I got divorced, there was an unexpected opportunity to sell the stable. It wasn't part of the plan, but it opened the door to something new … again. I was able to find a house with a small stable and a few acres of land. That chapter was quieter, more personal. A time of regrouping.

Since then, there have been a few more beginnings. I've been called a 'jack of all trades' and I think my shifting passions and string of new ventures are a perfect reflection of that. I've reconnected with my artistic side through photography, drawing, embroidery, crocheting and working with clay. These all came together when I opened a pottery/art studio. I enjoyed that adventure for five years. It blended creativity and connection in a way that felt really good, and for a while, it was exactly what I needed.

Not all beginnings are ones that you choose for yourself. A few years ago, my husband and I woke up in the dark of the early morning to discover our house was on fire. The entire story is too long to share here, but what I will say, is that it's another kind of beginning altogether. Letting go of what no longer remained and finding gratitude in what did.

Again, it was rebuilding day by day, one step at a time.

As much as we try to plan, sometimes the universe has other ideas, and things go in a different direction. It's good to remember that from the start, so that you can navigate the unexpected twists when they show up … and they usually do.

And then came another kind of beginning - writing my memoir.

To be honest, I argued with myself about doing it for years. Not because of timing or being too busy, but because I wasn't sure how much of the 'story' I was willing to tell. Or more accurately, how much I could tell without it affecting other people.

There were parts of my life that felt too tangled with others. Parts that didn't just belong to me. And I wrestled with that. A lot. But the story kept pulling at me. Quietly at first, and then louder. Until I realised I could write it in a way that honored both my truth *and* my integrity.

So ... I began.

With the guidance of my mentor and publisher, I was able to tell my story in the most honest way that I could, being careful with some parts, but not shying away from telling the truth of my experience. That was important ... and also freeing.

It turns out that sharing your story can create unexpected openings. Since publishing my memoir, I've had opportunities I never could have predicted. I've been invited to speak, contribute to other projects, and connect with people all over the world. And those opportunities came because I told the truth in my own words, in my own way.

One of those surprises? A moment I never saw coming - standing in Times Square, yes, *that* Times Square, the one in New York City - holding my own book in front of a billboard. A dream I never knew I had came true.

Telling my story has shown me a new level of feeling authentic. I believe that when you are able to really stay true to yourself, you become the most magnetic version of yourself. For years, I had wanted to share my stories, to hopefully inspire and connect with people. Little did I know that when that story was finally out in the world, an amazing new path would unfold. Looking back, it now feels a bit like 'ready or not, here I come.' But that's how it all works; when you honor your desires and take action to create them, the magic unfolds.

Writing my memoir helped me see just how many beginnings I'd already lived through - some chosen, some not. New businesses. New homes. A fire. A healing journey. Over and over, life has asked me to begin again.

And of course, not all beginnings were business-related. There have been personal ones too – going to college, taking flying lessons, moving from state to state (more than once).

And through it all, I started to notice something. I had instinctively been using tools that helped me move forward each time with more clarity. Things like deciding what I would and wouldn't tolerate. Choosing how I wanted to feel. Getting honest about what aligned with my values and what didn't. These were more than just preferences. They were my personal policies; my own set of inner agreements that helped me navigate new beginnings without losing myself in the process.

At the time, I didn't have a name for it. But eventually, those tools and truths formed the foundation of what I now call Queen Code Mastery™, my signature program. It's the framework I created from years of lived experience, unexpected plot twists and learning how to lead myself through it all.

Because when life throws you a new beginning – wanted or not – having your own code to return to can make all the difference.

It gives you a steady foundation to stand on when everything else is shifting.

It helps you make decisions with more confidence, communicate more clearly and trust yourself more fully. It doesn't mean life won't give you challenges, but it means you won't lose yourself in the process.

That's what Queen Code Mastery™ has become for me; a way to stay rooted, even when the path ahead is unknown. And now, it's something I share with others who are navigating their own beginnings, helping them create their own code, one that's aligned with who they are and where they're headed. If you've ever found yourself starting over, feeling untethered or unsure, personal policies can offer a sense of direction when nothing else feels clear.

# BEGIN IT NOW

Looking back now, I'm grateful for every messy, beautiful beginning. They shaped me into who I am, and who I continue to become.

All of this – the big changes, the smaller pivots, the unexpected twists – taught me that beginnings don't just bring excitement, sometimes they bring hesitation, fear or uncertainty. I've felt all of it. And I've learned that those feelings don't mean *you're doing it wrong*. They mean you're stepping into something new, something alive.

The thing is, not all beginnings are big and dramatic.

Some are loud, like a job change, a divorce or moving to a new city. But most are quieter. A new day. A fresh week. The first page of a journal. A shift in perspective. The decision to speak up. The moment you finally say 'enough' … or 'yes'… or even just 'maybe.'

They often show up disguised as ordinary moments. But if you're paying attention, you'll feel it; that tiny, inner nudge that says: *you can start here.*

Beginnings are everywhere. And that's what I've learned again and again.

You don't have to wait for the perfect time.

You don't have to have it all figured out.

You don't have to be ready.

You just have to begin.

What beginning is calling to you right now?

I love this quote by Theodore Roosevelt:

*'Do what you can, with what you have, where you are.'*

It's a great reminder that you don't need a perfect plan. You don't need certainty. Just a willingness to start from exactly where you are, with whatever tools, courage or desire you've got, and trust that the rest will come.

So whatever beginning is in front of you, whether it's bold and obvious or soft and quiet, trust yourself enough to take the first step. You don't have to be fearless. You just have to be willing. Begin it now … and see where it leads.

# LAURA MUIRHEAD

Laura Muirhead is an internationally acclaimed author, accomplished artist, and the CFO of her family's multi-million-dollar company. She is also the creator of the Queen Code program and the Queen Code Oracle Card Deck, which guide multi-passionate women to find clarity, set boundaries, and elevate both life and business, stepping into their full potential. Laura's work bridges creativity and business, demonstrating that success can be achieved on both sides of the spectrum.

Her personal journey is as dynamic as her professional life – she is a licensed pilot, an energy healer, and the author of *A Funny Thing Happened on the Way to My Life,* as well as a beloved children's book and three journals. Laura's life story is one of resilience and reinvention. From navigating the unexpected twists of life to rebuilding after a devastating house fire, she draws inspiration from her experiences to empower others.

Laura enjoys photography and exploring the world. She splits her time between homes in New Jersey and Michigan. Laura cherishes time with her husband, grown children, close friends, Labrador Retriever, and a life filled with creativity and adventure.

Website: afunnythinghappenedonthewaytomylife.com

# THE POWER OF STARTING

## LAURELLE JNO BAPTISTE

### A LOVE LETTER TO MYSELF (AND YOU)

It is never too late to stay true to yourself. Begin it now.

I was born on the small Caribbean Island of Dominica, where the population hovered around 70,000 - and my dreams often felt bigger than the land I walked on. During my time living there, opportunities felt limited. Conversations about technology, entrepreneurship and planning for the future were rare or almost nonexistent in my immediate environment. Yet, even amid those humble surroundings, I held onto something powerful - my imagination; it was boundless.

This is a love letter to the girl I was – and still carry within me. A person who refused to stop dreaming, who dared to begin again and again, even when the path was unclear. It's a gentle reminder that every setback holds the promise of a fresh start.

*Beginning*, I've come to learn, isn't about being ready. It's about being willing. Willing to grow, stumble, be misunderstood - and still show up. Still choose yourself. Still begin.

Wherever you are in life, whether you're returning to a dream or daring to imagine a new one – this is your moment. Begin it now.

## MY EARLY YEARS: QUIET SPARKS

As a child, I was blessed with an older sister who made me a student in her imaginary classroom. Most of her lessons focused on teaching me how to read and write with proper grammar. I didn't realise it then, but she was lighting the spark of a lifelong love of learning.

I was also surrounded by strong female teachers, and my mother. Women who stood tall, expected excellence, and made me feel seen. Because of them, I never questioned whether I could *become* something more. I believed the world would rise to meet my ambition.

But life has a way of testing belief. As I grew older, that early confidence wavered at times. I was often misunderstood and sometimes judged for dreaming too big. There were whispers and sideways glances. People thought I was trying to outshine them. But I wasn't. I was only ever in competition with the vision I held for myself.

I carried the weight of expectations that didn't fit who I was. Still, the fire inside me never truly went out. My desire to learn, to experience the world, to grow beyond what I could see, pulled me forward. And over time, I came to understand something deeply - *silencing your fire isn't safety, it's self-abandonment.*

So, I began again.

## BOLDNESS IN MOTION

Over the years, I've been blessed to travel the world, to meet people from different cultures, circumstances, and callings. I've learned that '*beginning*' never looks the same. For one person, it's going back to school. For another, it's leaving a job. For me, it was starting over in a place where I had no family, no safety net, no guarantees.

It was sitting alone at networking events. It was walking into rooms where I didn't look like anyone else ... and choosing to believe I still belonged.

# BEGIN IT NOW

Boldness isn't always loud. Sometimes, it's a whisper inside your spirit. Sometimes, it's a decision you make in private. It's showing up again, when no one claps. It's speaking your truth, even when your voice trembles.

Being bold means not letting fear lead the way. It means being intentional. It's becoming a light in a world that may try to dim your glow.

You don't need perfect conditions. You don't need a grand plan. You just need the courage to take the first step.

## BUILDING WHAT DOESN'T YET EXIST

My boldness also took shape through technology. I didn't just want to dream, I wanted to build. I found myself drawn to innovation, to solving complex problems, to designing systems that could make a real impact. Technology became my language for change. I began developing technology platforms, and leading digital transformation projects that help large-scale organisations navigate the future.

Working with these organisations gave me a bigger stage, but my mission remained the same - to build things that matter, to solve real problems, and to bring bold ideas to life. I found purpose at the intersection of vision and execution.

I'm passionate about using technology to create access - access to education, to opportunity, to empowerment. Whether it's launching enterprise systems or exploring the potential of artificial intelligence, I build tools that uplift people and transform industries. Innovation, for me, isn't about flashy breakthroughs, it's about thoughtful progress. About imagining what could be and then rolling up my sleeves to build it.

Along the way, I realised that driving innovation wasn't limited to product roadmaps or platform launches, it could also happen in a classroom. One of the most meaningful parts of that journey, was my time as a university lecturer. Standing in front of a classroom, guiding others through their own moments of beginning, was one of my greatest joys. There was something profoundly beautiful about witnessing someone step into their potential, watching their eyes light up as they realised they, too, could start. I didn't just teach content, I shared hope. I reminded students they had permission to dream and the power to act.

## WHEN DOUBT KNOCKS

If you dare to step outside the lines others have drawn for you, you will often meet resistance. People will question your choices. Some may even ridicule them.

We've all had moments when someone thinks they know us. When they assume they understand our choices, our motivations, even our dreams. Often, these assumptions come from people who've only seen pieces of our story, yet they speak with confidence about who we are and *what we should or shouldn't do*. It's a quiet pressure that can make us question ourselves.

Maybe it's when you left a "stable" job to pursue something that felt more meaningful. Or when you moved to a new city without a detailed plan - just a hope and a vision. Maybe you went back to school, started a business, or ended a relationship that no longer served who you were becoming. And suddenly, the questions came: *Are you sure this is a good idea? What if it doesn't work? Why would you give up something secure?*

These questions don't always come from malice. Sometimes they come from love, fear, or someone else's unresolved dreams. But with time, many come to learn that not every opinion deserves space in our journey. Other people's doubts, fears or limitations don't belong to us. We each have the right to grow, to begin again, and to follow a path that may not make sense to anyone else but feels deeply right to us.

It takes strength to stand tall in the face of that kind of noise. The judgments and projections of others aren't ours to carry and we don't have to take on what was never meant for us.

## IN THE COMPANY OF BEGINNINGS

There have been seasons where support was scarce, where the path felt lonely. But I moved forward anyway. And yet, through it all, I was never truly alone. I've been blessed to cross paths with incredible people - mentors, colleagues, partners, and friends - who understood the beauty and the cost of *beginning*. They were on their own journeys, navigating their own starts and restarts. Their support, whether through kind words, shared wisdom or simply walking beside me in silence, made a lasting impact. They reminded me that courage is contagious and that we rise more steadily when we rise together.

Each small act builds momentum. And that momentum builds confidence. And confidence builds growth.

The resistance we encounter from others often isn't truly about us, it's a reflection of others' uncertainties, their unspoken fears, or dreams they've set aside. When you move with purpose, you can unintentionally highlight what others haven't yet claimed for themselves. And while not everyone is ready for that light, it doesn't mean you should dim your own.

That's why boundaries are an act of self-respect. Surround yourself with those who cheer for your growth, who see your potential and want to see you rise. Your energy, your vision, your presence - they're valuable. Share them with those who uplift and inspire you in return.

Fear may show up on the journey, but it doesn't get to lead. Let it sit quietly in the backseat while you move forward anyway. Each step you take – starting something new, speaking up, learning something unfamiliar – is an act of courage that makes fear quieter and your confidence louder.

Confidence isn't something you stumble upon, it's something you create. You build it every time you follow through, every time you show up, every time you celebrate a small win. And even if no one else claps for you, notice your own growth, acknowledge your progress … and be proud.

The journey is yours and that's worth celebrating every day.

## HOW TO BEGIN, WHEREVER YOU ARE

Beginning doesn't need to be big. It just needs to be real.

Here are some gentle reminders for the journey:

Start small. Big dreams are built from tiny beginnings.

Share your dream wisely. Protect it until it's strong enough to stand.

Set goals, but don't be afraid to rewrite them. Begin as often as you need to.

Be kind to yourself. You are growing.

Redefine failure. It's not the opposite of success, it's part of it.

Keep moving. Step by step. Progress builds power.

Nourish your body, mind and soul.

Protect your peace. Who and what you allow in matters.

Choose yourself – daily, boldly, gently.

You don't need perfect timing. You don't need certainty. You just need to begin.

## THE TIME IS NOW

There was a time I thought I had to wait until I was ready, until the timing made sense, until the doubt disappeared. But I've learned that clarity often comes *after* the first step, not before it. And readiness? It's usually just a story we tell ourselves to stay safe.

I've started scared. I've started late. I've started over. More than once. And each time, something shifted; not all at once, not dramatically, but enough to remind me that movement is its own kind of magic.

Some days, I felt strong. Other days, I whispered my way forward, unsure but unwilling to stop. I've let go of things that felt familiar but no longer fit. I've said yes before I had a plan. And I've kept going, even when the applause was silent.

If you're holding something in your heart – a quiet idea, a hope you haven't said out loud, a version of yourself you're still becoming – I hope you give it room. I hope you begin, even if it's messy, even if it's small.

Because that's what I've done. And I'm still doing it.

With love,

Laurelle

# LAURELLE JNO BAPTISTE

Dr. Laurelle Jno Baptiste is a technology entrepreneur, innovator, and advocate for equitable access to education. As Chief Implementation Officer at Vocalmeet, she leads the development of technology platforms that help organizations streamline membership, events, regulatory affairs, finances, and online education through Vocalmeet's all-in-one solution — empowering member-based organizations to thrive in the digital age.

A university lecturer, speaker, and consultant, Dr. Jno Baptiste is a recognized expert in Agile project management and digital transformation. She has received multiple awards for innovation in technology and education, and she advises post-secondary institutions on digital learning strategies.

Holding a BSc in Computer Science, an MA, and a Doctorate in Education, she is dedicated to reshaping the future of education and professional development – ensuring that technology acts as an enabler, not a barrier, to success. As a trailblazer for women in tech, she remains committed to advancing inclusivity and making a global impact.

# FROM REFUGEE TO HUMANITARIAN

## LE THU PHAN-TRAN

### MY CHILDHOOD

I was born just before the 1968 Vietnam War, into a large family of fourteen children. My birth was unremarkable - just another girl among ten sisters and four brothers. I was the tenth child. When I fell seriously ill as a baby, my mother, fearing I wouldn't survive, rushed me to be baptised. I was named Thiên -Thu, meaning *Eternal Heaven*. Fearing they'd lose me to Heaven, my father changed my name to Lệ - Thu, meaning *Autumn Tears* - a name that carries gentleness, empathy and quiet strength.

My early years were joyful. Seeing all the abandoned Vietnamese-American children of the war without homes, my parents opened an orphanage and took them in. I spent my childhood growing up with orphans. We shared simple meals of soup, read together and slept side-by-side on the floor. My older sister taught me to read and write. They were happy days.

Everything changed in 1975, with the fall of Saigon. The Americans withdrew from the war bringing the orphans with them. Our family was meant to go with the orphans, but with two of my older sisters missing, my parents refused to leave without them. A few years later, I learnt that the plane with the orphans was shot down. This is why I have such a deep connection with children and orphans. Soon after, my father was imprisoned ... and life shifted into survival mode.

My mother, a devout woman, taught us more about faith than any book ever could. One night, with only one cup of rice left, a beggar knocked. She gave it away. I asked, 'What will we eat?' She said, 'We'll find leaves. What we give to others will last, but what we eat disappears.' Her unwavering kindness and faith in God came to be our anchor.

We scraped by, foraging in lakes and forests for food, collecting dead wood for cooking. I longed to attend school like the children I saw through the windows as we passed by. Birthdays weren't celebrated, and I had little sense of time or age - just the feeling of growing older.

## JOURNEY FOR FREEDOM

Years later, my father returned home; thinner and quieter. Once he gave me money to buy meat for a special family dinner. I rode my bicycle for hours to the open market but realised we could only afford shrimp. I remember feeling a quiet sadness that even a special meal was out of reach, not knowing that soon our family's struggle for survival would taken an even greater turn. Then came a string of mysterious nights, when my father and brothers returned home with buckets of fish. 'The boat is safe,' I overheard. But I didn't know what that meant at the time.

One morning at 3am, my mother and siblings left early for church, but my father told me to stay home with him. Soon after, neighbours crowded around our house taking everything that was outside. When they tried to break down the front door, my father told me to open it. When they saw me, they exclaimed, 'You haven't left yet?' and sheepishly returned everything. That's when I realised something bigger was happening. *Now I understand that night was a test drill for the real escape.*

Following suspicious rumours that our family was planning an escape, soldiers came and took my father for questioning. Fortunately, they didn't find any evidence of our escape plan and my sisters hid messages inside boiled vegetables to communicate this to my father, during their visits to the prison. *Our boat was safe for now.*

Eventually, he was released. One morning, again at 3am, our mother woke us and we quietly left our home. Instead of our usual route to Church, we boarded a small 4x10m wooden boat. We left behind the captain and the compass. As the sun rose, we took off at high speed, gunshots trailing behind us, until they faded into the distance. We were at sea.

For five nights, we drifted. I was too ill to eat and laid at the bow of the boat watching dolphins swim alongside. My father guided us by the stars, while my mother prayed her rosary day and night. In the near distance, we saw a ship. Hope surged but fell quickly as Thai pirates jumped aboard. Chaos erupted; everything blurred - footsteps, shouts, our muffled screams. I remember being dragged down to the bottom deck. It was dark, damp and heavy, with something I didn't have words for yet – *an unspeakable horror.* I remember trembling, disoriented, certain I was going to die. Shaken. Silenced. Stripped of safety and voice. I was fourteen years old. The next day, we ran from another ship, fearing more pirates, but the second pirate ship left our boat when they saw a submarine emerging from the surface.

Two days later, early in the morning, from a far distance we saw a tiny bird in the sky. We were overjoyed and the feeling was beyond words – WE WILL LIVE. My father wrote *SOS* on cardboard, but gunfire warned us to leave and a nearby boat motioned for us to follow. One by one we were led off the boat. I couldn't walk; I felt I was walking on air. A tall, very beautiful and kind American woman greeted us. My mother showed her a rubber stamp from the orphanage. Smiling, she arranged for a bus to take us to a hospital, where we had a hot shower. The doctor examined us, and after, we were given food and drink and taken to a very comfortable bed to rest the night. It was the most comfortable bed and the best sleep I'd had in a very long time.

The next day, we were moved to a small island; 'a refugee camp' awaiting to go to America. But when my parents saw the Australian ambassador, they asked if we could go to Australia and he agreed without hesitation. Autumn 1982, we arrived in Perth on a cold morning. We were taken to Graylands Hostel, and for the first time in my life, I felt an overwhelming sense of hope, as my family were together under one roof.

## NEW LIFE IN AUSTRALIA

Morning arrived with birds chirping, fresh clean cold air and blue sky. Warmly attired, we walked to have a scrumptious breakfast of toast, bacon, eggs, fruit juice … and a packed lunch to take to school. I loved school from the moment I sat in the front row. I remember singing the alphabet and learning from pictures. My first teacher, Mrs H saw the potential in me and moved me into a mainstream class after just one term. It was challenging, but I gave it everything.

Soon after, with help from the community, we moved to a small house in East Perth. We walked to St Mary's Cathedral, where we met Father Henry. He helped enrol us in St Thomas Aquinas, and the Dominican Sisters gave us uniforms, books and school bags. I was placed in Year 8, even though I had only just begun formal schooling at fourteen years old.

## STARTING MY EDUCATION

School was challenging. Not only was I not keeping up, I was often taken out of class to help my parents who needed me to translate for them. The Deputy Principal, Mrs R told my father to leave me at school. Many times, I wished I could be carefree like the other children and I wished I could understand everything the teachers said. With strong will and determination, I knew that *I must do well*, because education was my only chance for a better and brighter future. I dreamed of becoming a doctor and so was unrealistic when I chose to take the hardest subjects in year 11; physics, chemistry, and advanced maths. Seeing I was working very hard, but my results just didn't reflect my effort, my teachers advised me to change subjects to Economics and Accounting, to ensure an adequate score for my university entry.

Despite the hard work, I loved every moment of my school years, especially the kindness and love the Dominican sisters showed to me. Very often, I was excused from sport classes to spend time learning English with Sister Kath. She gave me a jumper when I first arrived at school cold, wearing just a shirt. A bowl of warm porridge was devoured quickly in the convent when Sister Kath knew I had no breakfast. These are precious memories, which instilled in me the unconditional love, compassion and kindness given to me when I needed it most.

During school holidays, to help bring in more income for my parents, I followed my older sisters to work nights in a fish factory and sew clothes during the day. On the weekends, my father asked me to help at the Vietnamese community to translate and fill out forms for anyone who needed help. In my final year of high school, my father opened a fish and chip shop. After school, we helped in the shop, then studied late into the night. I remember days before my TEE exams, studying through the nights and my mother bringing me water. I gave my all, and miraculously, I passed everything – except English, scoring just 49 for my TEE. My tears fell with overwhelming joy, as I called Sister Kath and took a bus to visit Sister Loreto, who took me to Curtin University to enrol.

Though my dream of becoming a doctor had faded, my strong desire to work in Health remained. I was looking for a career in Health Science and discovered the Bachelor of Applied Science (Medical Records

Administration). With reassuring words and an introduction from Sister Loretto to the head of school, Mrs. K, I was accepted into the course immediately.

## UNIVERSITY LIFE

Getting up early to catch two buses to university, and skipping breakfast most days, I suffered motion sickness from the long bus rides each day. I studied between lectures and tutorials in the library and sometimes stayed late for lectures, without food all day. Once, a friend told me I should be in a pie commercial because of the way I devoured one. I was starving.

In my second year, I met Quang - my first and only boyfriend. Quang was kind; often picking me up from university with a soft drink and muesli bar in hand. My father approved of him, provided he promised to support my studies. We were married a year later. University life was better, whilst Quang worked hard to bring an income, I continued to study. My results improved significantly.

## MY CAREER

In my final year, kindness was shown to me again, when Mrs. K recommended me for a part-time position as a Health Information Manager at a nursing home. I graduated in 1992 and began working full-time as a Clinical Coder. Whilst in the position, I sought out every opportunity acting in various positions including Health Information Manager, Release of Information Officer, and Decision Support Officer, all to gain experience. I was known for my work ethic. Working hard to save every dollar we could, and with the help of a surprise winning of $25,000 from a $2 scratchy, we built our first home in 1993. We had our two beautiful daughters in 1994 and 1998.

I believe with persistence, I not only learned a new language, but successfully completed high school and, against all odds, graduated from university with a degree in Health Information Management. This achievement was not just about academic success, it symbolised survival and proved that no obstacle is insurmountable with enough effort and determination.

**MY PHILANTHROPIC CALLING**
In 2006, one late evening, I was alone in the office working at Mercy Hospital Mount Lawley. The Mission Director, Amanda came to see me and said, "Le Thu, I am nominating you for the Catherine McAuley Award Developing Young Women into Leadership and Community Services. It's a one-year program opportunity for you to learn and be inspired by other amazing women in the world, who are making a difference in the community and to skill you up for leadership." I was speechless, excited, lost for words; in total disbelief that I was given this prestigious award. I know now, that this life-changing opportunity was divine will, to prepare me for who I am today in my philanthropic journey.

Reflecting on my life journey, *how could I not give back and love others unconditionally, when I have been given so much?* I would not be here today, had I not been given a chance for a new life, for an education that I thought I could only dream of, and for the love and support of countless people who have touched my life. I had seen the sacrifices my father made, the faith and the *lesson of giving to the beggar* my mother instilled in me and my childhood orphan friends.

The Catherine McCauley Award changed my life. Through retreats, workshops and powerful leaders, I saw the world in a broader light. I realised I wanted to give back - not just as a volunteer, but by creating something lasting. I was ready to make a difference, *but how could I do it?*

With flashbacks of my childhood, from hunger for education to days

I went to bed hungry, and the thought of my childhood orphan friends in the plane that was shot down, I asked my husband and our older friends to accompany me to return to Vietnam. We travelled from south to north to remote villages, where everything I saw was 'deja vu.' We met Father Sang and I was deeply moved by his programs, reaching out to the most vulnerable through funding cataract surgeries, academic scholarships, building compassion homes, and food hampers for the poor. When I returned home to Australia, I helped Father to organise musical concerts around Australia, raising funds.

For four years, I worked tirelessly to raise funds, but I felt my effort was like a drop of water in the ocean. The poor are everywhere, but my help felt limited. I thought, *by myself I can do very little, but if I have my own charity I can do much more*. And I would be responsible for the funds we raised and could make a greater impact.

## PROJECT HUMANITY AUSTRALIA INC

With my seventeen-years-old daughter, Victoria as a secretary, my parish priest Father Peter as my spiritual advisor, my lawyer friend Peter as Legal Advisor, Kevin as financial advisor, and some trusted acquaintances and colleagues on the management board, I founded Project Humanity Australia Inc in December 2011. To help make donations worthwhile, Peter and I worked hard over four years in our application for the tax-deductible scheme and we achieved DGR (deductable gift recipients) status in 2017. All board members are volunteers. Every dollar raised goes directly to the poor through our carefully assessed programs – helping those who needed it most.

## PROJECT HUMANITY AUSTRALIA INC: 2011 - 2025

Guided by Saint Teresa of Calcutta, *'If you can't feed a hundred people, then feed just one,'* I know firsthand what it feels like to receive food when

# BEGIN IT NOW

you're hungry or education when you never thought it possible. PHAI's projects focus on small, impactful acts:

- Compassion Kitchen - serving home cooked nutritious meals
- Compassion Classroom - for children without birth certificates
- Funding *scholarships* for academic gifted students to remain in school
- Distributing wheelchairs for children with disabilities
- Building Compassion Homes - especially for families with young children and elderly people
- Building *peppercorn and coffee plantations* providing long term income and self-sufficiency, as well as and *livestock programs* for community sustainability.
- Our Philanthropic Mission Trips offer firsthand experience of the struggles faced in these communities. They help our volunteers connect deeply with those we serve.

In fourteen years, our volunteers have worked tirelessly through fundraising events and in the Compassion Kitchen and Compassion Classroom. To date PHAI has provided over 213,000 nutritious meals, built 47 compassion homes, awarded over 1000 academic scholarships, distributed 1200 wheelchairs, medical funding for renal dialysis and children with cancer, Compassion Classroom for 58 students, built plantation for 32 families, livestock programs, distributed over 12,000 food hampers and 9 philanthropic mission trips.

**PROJECT HUMANITY AUSTRALIA INC: FUTURE VISION**
Children and the elderly hold a special place in my heart. Every child deserves nurturing, and every elder deserves dignity in their final years. PHAI's Mission is to focus on future empowerment – children, education and sustainable community development. Our Vision is a world

where every child has the opportunity to thrive, and every community has the tools to build a sustainable and dignified future.

## HOPE AND LEGACY

My journey has taught me that no matter where you start, with faith, determination and a commitment to your purpose, you can overcome even the greatest challenges.

Balancing work, family responsibilities and running a charity brought new complexities into my life. Yet, these experiences reinforced my commitment to transform personal struggles into a mission of hope for others. I learned that perseverance, discipline and a sense of purpose are critical to overcoming adversity. I transformed my hardships into a mission of hope - working not only to better my own life but to empower others.

Ultimately, my goal is not just to create change but to inspire others to believe in their ability to make a difference. By transforming adversity into motivation, I've made it my mission to empower others and address global challenges, proving that even the greatest obstacles can become opportunities for growth and transformation.

In 2025, I was honoured with third place in the *Women Changing the World – Humanitarian Impact People's Choice Award*.

Through faith, courage, and an unwavering belief in humanity, I strive to lead with compassion, empower the future, and inspire others to take that first step - to *Begin It Now*.

For more information, please visit website: www.projecthumanityaustralia.com

Donations (big or small) and Corporate Sponsors are always needed.

# LE THU PHAN-TRAN

Le Thu Phan-Tran was born in South Vietnam just before the 1968 Vietnam War, into a family of 14 children. Her early childhood was spent in an orphanage founded by her parents, where she lived until the fall of Saigon in 1975. With her father imprisoned during that time, Le and her younger siblings spent their days foraging for food in forests and lakes, and following their mother as she worked the family's small garden patch.

Le never had the chance to go to school. Instead, she watched longingly through classroom windows, dreaming of one day learning like the other children.

In 1981, shortly after her father was released from prison, the family built a small 4 x 10 metre boat and escaped Vietnam in search of freedom. With no captain, no compass, and only dried food and water, Le's family of 15 – along with 7 others – braved the open sea. They survived two encounters with pirates, relying on faith and the stars to guide them.

Le was just 15 when she arrived in Australia as a boat refugee. In a land full of opportunity – but speaking no English – she was determined to pursue the education she had always dreamed of. Her school years were far from typical. While her classmates focused on their studies, Le balanced learning with translating for her elderly parents as they adjusted to their new life.

Despite the challenges, Le graduated from Curtin University with a Bachelor of Science in Health Information Management. She went on to build a respected career and now works as a Health Information Manager for Ramsay Health Care, overseeing two private hospitals and bringing over 30 years of experience to the field.

In 2007, Le was selected for the Catherine McCauley Award Program, designed to develop young women into leaders and community advocates. After a year of mentoring by inspiring women changemakers, Le reflected deeply on her childhood hardships and her longing for education. It was then she began volunteering, fundraising, and joining philanthropic mission trips across Southeast Asia.

In 2011, with a vision that "alone I can do little, but with an organisation I can achieve much more," Le founded Project Humanity Australia Inc. (PHAi) with her 17-year-old daughter as secretary and a close group of friends on the Board.

As Founder and CEO, Le leads with empathy, courage, and a strong belief that even the smallest act of kindness can transform lives. Inspired by Mother Teresa's words, "If you can't feed 100 people, then feed just one," Le's mission continues to grow.

PHAi has reached hundreds of thousands of lives across Southeast Asia and Australia through its initiatives—Compassion Kitchen, Compassion Homes, academic scholarships, medical support for children, gift distribution, sustainable agriculture and livestock programs, and education access through Compassion Classroom.

In 2025, Le was honoured as a finalist in the Women Changing the World Global Awards, taking third place in the Humanitarian Impact People's Choice Award.

With faith, courage, and a deep belief in humanity, Le is committed to building a legacy that inspires others to take action—and to Begin It Now.

# RISING FROM ROCK BOTTOM

## A GUIDE TO REDEFINING YOUR DESTINY

### PARVINA MIRAKHMEDOVA

In my experience of communicating with people from various walks of life, most believe that individuals are born either 'under a lucky star' or as a 'loser' - and that there are no other options for one's destiny besides these two.

The country you're born in and the family you come from, rich or poor, are considered so crucial, that everything else seems insignificant. Whether you're intelligent, brave or possess a unique perspective on the world - it just seems to lose its meaning. After living 36 years of a very full life, abundant in sorrows yet ultimately more joys and triumphs, I want to share how to achieve success, regardless of your country or family background.

There are 7 fundamental principles that have made me who I am and brought me to where I am today.

## PRINCIPLE 1 – DETERMINE HOW YOU SEE THE WORLD

I'm sure everyone has experienced apathy and depression, when the whole world seems grey, has lost all its colour, and you simply stop noticing the joy in life, seeing miracles, or encountering adventures. But the world itself doesn't change just because we think differently about it – only we can decide which bright or dark sides of the world we choose to notice right now.

My friend, who doesn't live lavishly and doesn't own her home, found a sick puppy near her house. This wasn't the first animal she decided to help, despite her own difficulties and the fact that all her finances were going towards house repairs, after the destructive actions of her other 'street-rescued' pets.

She couldn't take it in, as her home was already full of adopted pets. She teamed up with the neighborhood children to build it a little home and feed it before she left for work. When she returned, the puppy was gone. Some 'helpful' stranger had taken it away and abandoned it elsewhere. My friend was heartbroken, as finding the puppy felt impossible. Despite this, she refused to hate the world, even if, to her, it felt like only the lovely and perfect puppies could truly thrive.

Just two days later, a friend from a different part of the city messaged her a photo of a sick puppy she'd discovered, requesting her assistance with its treatment. Can you imagine her shock when she saw it was THAT VERY SAME PUPPY!

Clearly, a higher power had directed it to another compassionate soul!

Imagine how wonderful and magical the world appeared to my friend, and to all who heard this story.

*By continuing to see the bright side of the world (without ignoring the dark ... (because, let's face it, we don't live in a perfect world!) people perform acts of unimaginable bravery, courage, creativity and compassion, generating an enormous amount of good that ALWAYS comes back to them - in one way or another.*

## PRINCIPLE 2 – PEOPLE LEAVE YOUR LIFE EXACTLY WHEN THEY'RE MEANT TO

Loss is a universal experience; everyone faces the departure of loved ones. Whether someone passes away, moves away and loses contact, or a friendship simply fades over time, the result is the same. We all grapple with sadness, disappointment and the profound ache of trying to mend the hole left by their absence.

I'll share my own experience. My father passed away from cancer when he was only 48 years old. To this day, tears well up whenever I talk, or write, about it. The truth is, he's no longer physically by my side. However, all his advice and guidance remain firmly in my mind. They haven't vanished, and no one can take them from me - unless, of course, with a lobotomy.

You might wonder; why this specific title for the section? It's because *I truly believe my dad's departure was exactly when he was meant to leave.*

I don't know *why* this was the most appropriate time, but who I've become is undeniably linked to his leaving. He raised me to be a good person, helped me become independent, and then he was gone. Perhaps this idea will be unclear to many, but when you face the loss of someone (and it doesn't have to be their death), you'll eventually understand that THEY HAD TO LEAVE.

*Time softens the sting of sadness, bitterness and disappointment, letting us continue to live our own lives - which is precisely what we're meant to do. While the hole in our chest may never fully close, it gradually fills with the blossoms of our thoughts and the triumphs of our achievements, becoming cherished shared memories.*

**PRINCIPLE 3 – FALLING MAY FEEL UNSETTLING, BUT ONLY YOU HAVE THE POWER TO CATCH YOURSELF – AND BEGIN TO RISE. THE CONTROL RESTS FIRMLY IN YOUR HANDS**
Imagine being on a pedestal, showered with praise, the most wanted presence at every school, university, or work event. Yet, recall Principle 1; the world inherently possesses both bright and dark aspects. Suddenly,

you're not the favorite, and no one seems to care. (Think of any moment in your life … I'm certain you'll find one.)

This is my story. I was a highly qualified eye doctor, with numerous awards and diplomas, when suddenly I lost function in my left wrist. Overnight, it felt like no one cared. My employer, while expressing regret, fired me. It wasn't personal - just business. I then lost my father, and my mother became seriously ill. I was let go because I could no longer perform my duties as a physician.

I once asked a psychologist; 'How should a person feel in such a situation?' And here is the answer I received, which is totally true:

'In such a situation, a person likely experiences a complex mix of intense emotions. Initially, there would be profound shock and disbelief at the sudden loss of physical function, especially for a highly skilled professional like an eye doctor. This would quickly turn into fear and anxiety about the future - loss of career, financial instability and the sheer uncertainty of what comes next.

The employer's decision, while framed as "just business," would undoubtedly sting, leading to feelings of betrayal, anger, and resentment. Perhaps even a sense of being discarded, despite past achievements. This can deeply wound one's self-worth and identity, especially when a significant part of that identity was tied to their profession and accomplishments. It is very sad, is it not?'

But just like the experience with the puppy, it felt as if a higher power intervened, guiding me to work that allowed me time to recover and regain my self-esteem. I still feel gratitude for the unexpected help, a renewed sense of purpose, and immense pride in my ability to overcome adversity and achieve recognition … even with continued physical limitations. This journey from rock bottom to significant achievement fostered deep feelings of strength and personal validation.

Yes, my wrist still does not function, yet recently, I was honoured with a prestigious award in London for my scientific work and my life's journey, and recognised as *an Alien of Extraordinary Ability* by the USA.

Tell me, what emotions have gripped you in your darkest hour? Was it boiling anger, raw indignation, deep resentment, an overwhelming urge to scream ... or the contrary desire to vanish into the most private corner and weep endlessly?

Know this: *all these feelings are natural ... until they lead you to consider harming anyone, yourself included.* That's the critical point. This is the exact moment to pivot, to begin moving in the opposite direction, and to actively redefine the world around you.

*Always remember, the course of your life - whether forward or backward, upward or downward - rests solely in your hands.*

## PRINCIPLE 4 – REMEMBER YOUR GENIUS

In a world saturated with images of 'success' screaming from every screen, it's dangerously easy to succumb to societal pressures and trendy notions of what a 'successful person' looks like. Social media, in particular, relentlessly parades the *successful success of a successful person*. Suddenly, you find yourself doubting everything you were once told in school; those moments you were praised for a brilliantly written essay or a well-executed project. You begin to question your mother's words, who always speaks of her wonderful son or daughter, and gradually, you start to believe in your own worthlessness. Sound familiar?

I want to assure you, my dear friend - *this is nothing but illusion*. Switch off the internet, for then you would never even know about that successful singer launching their cosmetic line. If we all had to unsubscribe from that popular blogger, they would suddenly become irrelevant to sponsors. This kind of success is fleeting.

We - you and I - are the architects of our success.

Instead, it is YOUR INNATE GENIUS to perceive and cultivate

talent in others, to approach your work with unparalleled professionalism, and to subtly inspire a kinder outlook towards the vulnerable in everyone you meet.

*So much could be said about true genius, about YOUR true genius, but you seem to have forgotten it. Guard that flame. Don't let anyone extinguish the brilliance of your genius.*

*You are a genius.*

## PRINCIPLE 5 – TRUST YOUR INSTINCT! WHEN YOU FEEL LIKE SOMETHING HAS CHANGED, YOU'RE NOT IMAGINING IT

You've been at the same job for years. Teams change, projects pivot, and suddenly, you feel it - something's off. At first, you tell yourself it's just exhaustion, burnout, and you're convinced a vacation will fix everything. Yet, after your break, you realise it's only gotten worse. This place, you now understand, simply doesn't give you the same sense of joy or purpose it once did.

'It's just a job,' some will say. 'It's not supposed to be positive, just pay the bills.' But the truth is, the atmosphere around us, in every aspect of our lives, feeds or starves the flame of our genius and our self-belief.

It's like a prized garden flower - without the right humidity and temperature, it withers, losing its beauty for the gardener. So too, when you feel a change, you need to assess if this new 'climate' truly sustains you, if it nurtures your self-belief, or if it's slowly snuffing out your brilliant flame. If your gut says, 'No, this isn't right for me,' then you already know your next step … no matter how terrifying it seems.

Take for instance, a colleague of mine who married for love. At first, all was well. She overlooked some changes in her husband's behavior (occasional fits of jealousy), interpreting them as signs of his intense love for her.

After some time, she moved to a different country, far from her parents. Due to circumstances, she had to start working, despite having a small child, because her husband couldn't find 'suitable' work. Her husband's jealousy increased to round-the-clock, becoming unbearably toxic, giving her no room to breathe. He would come to her workplace to 'try and catch her cheating' with a colleague.

My colleague realised she was constantly feeling guilty for her husband's jealousy, and that she had become a laughingstock in society. Most importantly, *she stopped feeling like herself.* Her self-belief weakened and the flame of her own genius began to fade.

Finally, one pivotal day, she found the strength to say STOP and filed for divorce. Her husband's threats of physical harm couldn't deter her; she persevered.

Now, she is a thriving specialist in her industry, generously contributing the full harvest of her genius to the world.

*Walking away - from a spouse, from a job - isn't a catastrophe. More often than not, it is a vital act of self-preservation and strength. Listen to that quiet voice inside you—the one telling you something has changed. It isn't doubt; it is your truest self-calling you to act. Your instinct is your compass, and your life's greatest adventures begin the moment you decide to follow it.* So, TRUST YOUR INSTINCT!

## PRINCIPLE 6 – SEIZE THE CHANCE: DO SOMETHING TO MOVE TOWARDS YOUR GOAL EVERY DAY

*They say that opportunity knocks when you're ready for it.*

My friend, who was carrying her third child, and with her two other children in tow, journeyed to a land promising great opportunity. There, she reunited with a husband who had no steady job or stable home. Her fervent hope was to bring their family back together; to confront all hardships side-by-side. Their marriage hung by a thread, on the verge of collapse from internal turmoil, and only this desperate move to join him offered a chance at salvation.

She faced rebuilding her life from the ground up; navigating a new country unfriendly to immigrants, battling to get her children into school, enduring a high-stress birth for her healthy baby, compiling critical documents and seeking citizenship. This exhaustive journey spanned several years - a period defined by profound suffering, persistent anxiety and overwhelming stress, which took a significant toll on her health.

With these immense challenges finally behind her, only one, deeply held, yet elusive dream remained - to return to her profession; to be a doctor. Nations worldwide have unique requirements for legitimising foreign medical degrees, and in this specific country, those demands were exceptionally stringent.

My friend began to prepare for her exams daily, studying whenever she could, while her youngest child slept and her older children were at school. Then, suddenly, all the testing centers closed due to the country's political situation. When they finally reopened, it was only in a few select cities, and booking slots became a fierce race against time, available only at specific hours. This setback delayed my friend from taking her exam for another year.

Yet, she never faltered in her daily attempts to secure an exam slot, all while remaining an exceptional mother to her children. And then, finally, she booked it … and passed the exam in a very short time!

Now, she is a certified specialist in that once-foreign country!

*She proved that the main thing is not to miss your chance, and to do at least a little something every day towards YOUR goal.*

*Was it scary? Yes!*
*Was it hard? Very!*
*But did she do it? Absolutely!*
*And so can you!*

The Last and Most Important Point:

## PRINCIPLE 7 – IT IS LOVE, NOT FEAR, THAT TRULY MOTIVATES

There isn't a single thing on Earth stronger than love. It's what truly motivates us to achieve great things. The love of God, the love of parents, the love of your partner, of children, of friends - this is an endlessly replenishing energy that allows us to overcome all problems and drives us forward.

So, I'll leave you with this final thought … just for you. When love is your driving force, the impossible begins to feel possible. And with the principles above on your side, success isn't just waiting – it's already on its way to you.

# PARVINA MIRAKHMEDOVA

Dr. Parvina Mirakhmedova, born in Dushanbe, Tajikistan in 1989, is a distinguished ophthalmologist and groundbreaking innovator dedicated to advancing eye care.

A top graduate of Avicenna Tajik State Medical University (ATSMU) with honors, Dr. Mirakhmedova was a recipient of the prestigious Presidential Scholarship. She played a pivotal role in pioneering intravitreal bevacizumab injections in Tajikistan, significantly contributing to preventing blindness and improving vision for countless patients.

Her prolific scientific contributions include 19 authored and co-authored publications in Scopus-indexed journals and presentations at international conferences. Her research has notably focused on improving the early diagnosis of primary open-angle glaucoma, particularly through the evaluation of retinal nerve fiber layer thickness, addressing crucial diagnostic gaps.

Dr. Mirakhmedova's innovative spirit led to the development of two significant proposals for improving diagnostics:

A new method for quantifying anterior chamber inflammation via software, significantly enhancing objective assessment in conditions like uveitis.

# PARVINA MIRAKHMEDOVA

An innovative proposal for diagnosing glaucoma using software, aimed at improving early detection and management.

These pioneering software-based methods, presented with acclaim in January 2025 at the Congress of the Ophthalmology Society of Tajikistan, earned her international recognition, including the Golden Heart Award (presented by the Duchess of York) and the Gold Tech Innovation Award at the 2025 Women Changing The World Awards in London. She also received the Best Young Scientist of the Year 2025 prize in Kazakhstan for her software-based inflammation assessment.

Beyond her clinical and scientific breakthroughs, Dr. Mirakhmedova actively shapes the future of ophthalmology and medical education. She has served as Head Ophthalmologist at Nurafzo Diagnostic Center LLC, building its department from scratch. She was an Assistant Editor-in-Chief of the Simurgh medical journal and, in 2024, joined a four-member expert commission to develop a new ophthalmology curriculum for Khatlon State Medical University, aligning it with national education standards. In April 2024, her expertise was recognized when she served as a jury member evaluating ophthalmologists in a scientific competition in Dushanbe. Her dedication to public health was further demonstrated by chairing a Medical Commission that provided primary ophthalmological care to nearly 12,000 children in rural areas of Tajikistan.

Dr. Mirakhmedova's career highlights her exceptional professionalism, clinical excellence, and profound impact on global health through innovation and leadership.

In May 2025, Dr. Parvina Mirakhmedova received approval for the Alien Worker petition (EB-1A) and is now officially recognized in the United States as an Alien of Extraordinary Ability. This designation is granted to individuals with exceptional achievements and recognition in their professional field.

# A JOURNEY FROM DESPERATION TO PASSION

## RAND ALKISHTAINI

I was born into a family where the image of *a perfect mother* served as my guiding star. My mom, a paragon of grace and warmth, effortlessly managed our home with an unparalleled elegance. She was not just a great housewife, she was a creative force, known for her exceptional taste in house styling. Our living room was a canvas of her artistry, often adorned with the latest issues of House & Garden magazine, their glossy pages filled with inspiration. As a child, I absorbed her values and aesthetics, as well as the quiet strength she exuded. I dreamed of becoming the ideal housewife she embodied, but little did I know that these early influences would shape my journey in ways I could never have imagined.

At the tender age of 22, I embarked on the next chapter of my life … when I got married. My dream then was to create a loving family, to nurture and build a home just like the one I grew up in. After graduating with a BSc in IT, I felt a sense of readiness as I moved to the Gulf Cooperation Council (GCC), full of hope and excitement for this new adventure. The culture was vibrant and diverse, and I was eager to immerse myself in this new environment. My life took a transformative turn when, just two years into my marriage, I welcomed my first daughter into the world. The moment she arrived, my dream of becoming a mother blossomed into reality, filling my heart with joy and purpose.

As I cradled my newborn in my arms, I felt an overwhelming sense of love and responsibility. Motherhood was everything I had envisioned; a beautiful, chaotic whirlwind of sleepless nights, endless nappy changes, and precious milestones. However, as the years rolled on, a growing sense of restlessness began to creep in. Motherhood, while fulfilling, awakened a deeper yearning within me, an inner energy that sought expression beyond the confines of my domestic life. It was during this tumultuous phase that I faced one of the most challenging periods of my life. I felt lost and hopeless, questioning my identity beyond the roles of wife and mother.

In those dark moments, I was fortunate to have a supportive family who rallied around me, encouraging me to step outside my comfort zone. They recognised the flicker of ambition in me and pushed me to explore new avenues. Their faith in me was a lifeline, and their encouragement ignited a desire to rediscover myself. With their support, I decided to enroll in various classes aimed at self-discovery. This journey began with a course in another country, that required me to commute every two weeks. I felt a mixture of excitement and anxiety as I prepared for this new chapter.

The experience turned out to be a pivotal moment in my life. It forced me to confront my fears and embrace the unfamiliar. Each commute was a journey, not only across borders, but also within myself. I met people from diverse backgrounds and listened to their stories, which enriched my perspective on life. This immersion into a new environment opened my eyes to possibilities I had never considered. I remember the exhilaration I felt, stepping into the classroom where I was surrounded by like-minded individuals, all eager to learn and grow.

One particular lesson stands out vividly in my memory. On that first day, as we introduced ourselves, I hesitated, downplaying my accomplishments, identifying myself solely as a mother and housewife. My professor, a wise and perceptive man, sensed my self-doubt. He challenged me in front of the class, saying, 'She believes being a mum and a housewife doesn't make her an extraordinary woman.' His words struck a chord within me, awakening a realisation that my identity was not limited to my domestic roles. It was a revelation that set me on the path of exploration.

Over the next decade, I delved into various fields, each experience unraveling new layers of my identity. It was a journey marked with trials and errors, but each step brought me closer to understanding my true self. I took courses in art, design and even entrepreneurship, all adding a new thread to the tapestry of my life. I experimented with different mediums, discovering a love for colour, texture and form. It was liberating to express myself creatively, and with every project, I became more empowered.

Finally, after years of exploration and self-discovery, I chose to become a certified interior decorator. I was excited but also apprehensive. Venturing into this new field felt like stepping into the unknown, and uncertainty loomed over me as I took this leap. I didn't know what the future held, but I adopted a philosophy of taking small, calculated steps, ensuring that if I stumbled, the damage would be minimal. Each project I took on was approached with care, allowing me to grow and learn with every endeavor.

Then, when the pandemic hit in 2020, I feared that my budding career as a decorator would come to a screeching halt. The world was in chaos, and many businesses faced unprecedented challenges. I watched as friends and colleagues grappled with uncertainty, and felt a wave of anxiety wash over me. However, I quickly realised that instead of succumbing to fear, I could use this time to innovate and adapt. The constraints of lockdown forced me to think outside the box, and I turned inward, tapping into my creativity.

During this time, I was inspired to reimagine my work. I decided to incorporate art into my designs, creating pieces that were both functional and artistic. I began experimenting with colours and textures, blending different styles to create unique designs that resonated with my vision. This new direction fueled my passion and allowed me to hone my design skills through various classes and workshops. I immersed myself in learning, reading books, watching tutorials, and seeking mentorship from established artists and designers. Each lesson was a steppingstone, pushing me further along my path.

After two years practicing my craft, I began exhibiting my designs both locally and internationally. The thrill of showcasing my creations to the world was indescribable. My brand expanded to include home accessories, and I found myself in a whirlwind of creativity and success. The response from the public was overwhelmingly positive, and I felt a sense of validation for all the hard work I'd put in. Today, as I write my story, I am filled with gratitude for the journey that has brought me here.

I have received accolades, including the Artistic Luminary Award and the Poul Henningsen Award for Outstanding Product Design. Additionally, being selected as one of the top three nominees in the Art & Design category for the Women of the Year 2024 in Bahrain, as well as winning an honorable mention for the Women Changing the World Global Award 2025 in the Creative Industries category; which has been profoundly humbling. Each recognition serves as a reminder of the journey I embarked on, the obstacles I overcame and the dreams I dared to chase.

Reflecting on my journey, I realise that the path has not been linear. There were moments of doubt and times when I questioned whether I was making the right choices. But each challenge taught me invaluable lessons, which I now impart to every new mother and housewife - it's never too late to pursue your dreams. Embrace the joys of motherhood and cherish the time spent with your children, but don't forget to invest in yourself. Learning new skills and understanding your passions will prepare you for the moment when your dreams can take flight.

I began my career in my late thirties, but I have no regrets. I was present for my children during their formative years, and I treasure every moment spent with them. I learned to seize opportunities as they arose, understanding that life is a series of moments that shape who we are. My experiences have shown me that life often has a plan for us that we can't yet see. I encourage those who feel lost or unsure of their goals to explore every opportunity that presents itself. You may fail, but each setback is a steppingstone toward success. Embracing failure as part of the journey will strengthen you and teach you valuable lessons.

As I reflect on my definition of success, I realise that it has evolved over the years. Initially, success for me was rooted in personal growth and self-fulfillment. Then it transitioned to recognition from others, and now it encompasses financial stability and independence. Each stage of success is significant, and I encourage everyone to follow their dreams patiently. Life is not solely about creating a career, it's about crafting a fulfilling existence.

In closing, I urge you to always prioritise your family while remembering to nurture your own aspirations. It's essential to strike a balance between your roles as a mother and an individual. Success is a journey, not a destination. Embrace it, cherish every moment, and never hesitate to pursue your dreams. You never know where your path may lead, but trust that it will be worth every step. As I continue on my journey, I carry with me the lessons learned and the joy that comes from pursuing a life filled with purpose and passion.

So, to all the mothers and housewives out there — your dreams matter. It's never too late to start. Take that first step, embrace the unknown, and allow yourself to grow. You are extraordinary, and your journey is just beginning.

# RAND ALKISHTAINI

Hello! I'm Rand Alkishtaini, an Iraqi-born interior decorator and artistic designer with a passion for creating beautiful, functional spaces. Born in Baghdad in 1982, I was raised between Jordan and Canada. I have been living in the Gulf Cooperation Council (GCC) for over 20 years. I'm excited to share my journey with you – it's been a remarkable adventure filled with challenges and discoveries that have shaped who I am today.

My career path was not always clear. I earned a Bachelor's degree in IT, but despite my education, I never found fulfillment in that field. This led me to a profound realization that took 13 years to unfold: my true passion lies in interior design and art. During a challenging period of my life, which I refer to as my "desperate housewife" stage, I grappled with uncertainty and a longing for self-discovery. This phase, while tough, pushed me to work harder and develop my skills, ultimately guiding me toward my creative outlet.

I have been honored to receive the Artistic Luminary Award, recognizing my contributions to design. Additionally, I was nominated as one of the top three finalists for the Woman of the Year Award in the Art and Design category in Bahrain and was a winner of the Women

Changing the World Global Award in the Creative Industries category. These achievements are powerful reminders of the resilience I've built through my journey and fuel my passion to inspire others.

Today, I am the proud founder of Vintage House Decor in Bahrain, where I specialize in creating unique and artistic interior designs that blend functionality with beauty. My work is about transforming spaces into reflections of personal stories and experiences. I am also actively involved in the Bahrain Art Society and the Bahrain Businesswomen Society, collaborating with fellow artists and entrepreneurs to promote creativity and innovation within our community.

In addition to my design work, I serve as the Vice President of Public Relations at the Voice of Innovators Toastmasters Club. This role allows me to connect with diverse individuals, enhancing my communication skills while helping others develop their own. I believe effective communication is vital in both personal and professional spheres, and I am passionate about fostering an environment where ideas can flourish.

My journey has taught me that it's never too late to pursue your dreams. I encourage everyone, especially women and mothers, to embrace their aspirations and invest in themselves. Life is a series of moments, and each one is an opportunity for growth and discovery. As I continue to explore my creative passions, I remain committed to inspiring others to unlock their potential and follow their

I look forward to sharing more of my experiences and insights with you!"

# THE FIFTY-DOLLAR AWAKENING

## HOW FINANCIAL CRISIS BECAME MY GREATEST TEACHER

### RANIA AL KHUSAIBI

In a world where financial success is measured by numbers alone, I invite you to look deeper. This chapter is not merely about money; it's about self-discovery, resilience and reclaiming your power through mindful money management. My journey began with an obstacle that became the spark for my life's mission – to support others in achieving financial peace of mind.

At twenty years old, I found myself broke, in a foreign country, overwhelmed by shame and dependence. Today, I am a financial educator, entrepreneur and advocate, who has helped hundreds transform their relationship with money. The path between these two realities wasn't paved with luck, it was built through intentional choices, emotional healing and the courage to begin.

Through personal stories, hard-won lessons, and practical wisdom, I hope to inspire you to take your first step – no matter where you are – towards a future of financial freedom and inner calm. Because the truth I've discovered is this; financial peace isn't about having more money, it's about making peace with the money you have and building systems that serve your deepest values.

## THE AWAKENING – THE MOMENT EVERYTHING CHANGED

At twenty years old, I embarked on what should have been the most exciting chapter of my life; pursuing my education abroad. As the daughter of loving parents in Oman, I had been sheltered from financial realities. Being one of four girls, I was perhaps spoilt in ways that left me unprepared for the practical demands of independent living. Money had always appeared when needed and budgeting was never discussed at our dinner table.

Within my first month away from home, poor financial management left me completely broke. Standing in my small student accommodation wondering what I should do, I felt the crushing weight of failure. It wasn't just that I had no money, I felt I had let myself and my parents down. I was twenty years old and couldn't manage one month of expenses … what a failure!

Desperate and too embarrassed to ask my father for help (knowing it would take at least three days for money to transfer in those pre-digital banking days), I borrowed AU$50 from a friend. What should have been a simple favour, quickly became humiliating when he demanded repayment in a disrespectful and demeaning manner. In that moment of vulnerability and shame, I made a quiet but fierce vow to myself – never again would I be financially dependent on anyone.

I had no idea that this moment would become the cornerstone of my life's calling in financial empowerment.

The pain of that experience taught me that financial illiteracy isn't a character flaw, it's simply a gap in education. Many of us, particularly those from protective family environments, reach adulthood without basic money management skills. The shame we feel isn't deserved but it is

# BEGIN IT NOW

an opportunity for growth.

That moment of borrowing money could have broken my spirit permanently. Instead, it ignited a determination to never again be at someone else's financial mercy. The key was transforming embarrassment into education, dependence into self-reliance.

What felt like personal failure became the foundation for helping hundreds of others. Sometimes our deepest wounds become our most powerful platforms for service.

From that day forward, I began educating myself about money. I devoured every financial book I could find, enrolled in workshops whenever possible, and transformed every experience into a learning opportunity. Though finance wasn't my degree subject, my tendency to hyper-focus on things I'm passionate about, meant I became my own most dedicated teacher.

My friends would marvel, often joking, 'How come you always have money? You're never broke.' They had no idea how seriously I had taken that vow to never lack money again. Behind their casual observation lay countless hours of intentional learning and disciplined action.

I worked multiple part-time jobs - as a waitress, radio host and charity worker – not just for the income, but for the invaluable life education they provided. Serving tables taught me about customer service and working under pressure. Radio hosting developed my communication skills and confidence. Charity work connected me to purpose beyond personal gain. Each role offered lessons I would never have learnt in a classroom, skills that would later prove essential in my entrepreneurial journey. For this unexpected education, I remain profoundly grateful.

## RECLAIMING DIGNITY THROUGH DISCIPLINE – THE FOUNDATION OF FINANCIAL PEACE

With my first full-time job, I made deliberate choices that seemed unusual for a woman in her early twenties. I created detailed monthly budgets, steered clear of loans, and prioritised saving, even when it meant sacrificing social opportunities. I wasn't just managing my money, I was reclaiming my dignity and building unshakeable peace of mind.

I discovered that *financial independence* isn't about having excess wealth, it's about having the power to make life choices without money being the determining factor. I often remember saying no to expensive social gatherings, avoiding impulse purchases and tracking every cent I spent. These habits felt restrictive to friends but were transformative for me.

Even after meeting my soon-to-be-husband, I maintained these disciplines. My friends were shocked when I chose not to have an elaborate wedding party; a significant cultural expectation in our society. By then, I had learned the difference between spending to impress others and spending to enrich my own life. For me, the meaning of a rich life is one where you align your money with your values, investing in what truly brings you joy, not social approval.

As financial guru Dave Ramsey says, '*I chose to live like no one else, so I could later live like no one else.*'

Instead of a lavish celebration, I gifted my husband-to-be a combined budget template. He was surprised, at first, but soon came to appreciate how thoughtful and empowering financial planning can be.

The deeper work, however, was emotional. I began journaling my earliest memories of money, asking myself where I had learned to associate spending with guilt or saving with selfishness. I confronted my fear of being judged for having financial boundaries and gave myself permission to define success on my own terms.

Creating and maintaining budgets, saving consistently and making intentional spending choices are powerful forms of self-care. They show that you value your future self enough to make thoughtful choices today.

Did it mean I didn't enjoy life? Absolutely not! It meant I got to enjoy it on my own terms, spending on what truly brought me joy, without the pressure to impress or meet others' expectations. That's real freedom.

Living in a Gulf country with expectations around expensive weddings, luxury cars, designer brands and impressive homes, I had to actively choose my own definition of success over society's version. This required both courage and clarity about my true values.

One powerful breakthrough came when I asked myself: 'If my sons grew up to handle money the way I do, would I be proud?' That question changed everything. I wanted them to feel confident, not anxious; empowered, not ashamed. So, I had to embody that first. I wanted them to understand that while money does not necessarily give you happiness, it does give you options!

**FROM PERSONAL JOURNEY TO PUBLIC MISSION**
The COVID-19 pandemic served as a wake-up call for many, coupled by Oman's significant changes in government structure that affected jobs and benefits. As jobs were lost and incomes reduced, I watched friends and colleagues struggle to make ends meet. Though I was financially stable, I felt the emotional weight of their stress and uncertainty.

Friends came to me for advice. That's when I realised my personal financial journey could serve a much larger purpose. I began by sharing my story and lessons on social media. What started as simple tips soon evolved into workshops, consultations and, eventually, a comprehensive mission. I wanted to teach others what I wish I had known at a young age: *how to build a healthy relationship with money.*

I focused particularly on empowering Arab youth and women, having discovered during my research, a stark lack of accessible, simplified financial content in Arabic. Not investment advice or get-rich-quick schemes, but foundational knowledge forming the basis of lifelong financial wellness that is given in very simple and relatable language. Many families in Gulf countries tend to shelter their children, money often being a taboo subject, with the expectation that young people should focus solely on studies and only consider employment after university. Part-time jobs during summers are still not common, so many university students have never managed money independently.

One woman stayed behind after a workshop session, tears filling her eyes as she said, 'I've always thought I was irresponsible with money. But now I realise I just didn't know how. No one ever taught me.' That moment crystalised my understanding. So many people weren't making poor decisions, they simply weren't given the knowledge, language or safe space to learn.

What begins as individual healing, often evolves into collective service. The skills and insights you develop through your own struggles become resources for helping others navigate similar challenges.

Providing accessible, culturally relevant financial education - especially to underserved communities – creates ripple effects of empowerment that extend far beyond individual bank accounts. When I couldn't find comprehensive financial education in Arabic, I created it myself! Often, the gap you identify in your own journey reveals the service the world needs from you.

My credibility as a financial educator didn't come from having vast wealth, but from having navigated real challenges and developed practical systems that worked. Authenticity resonates more than perfection.

## BUILDING SYSTEMS THAT SCALE – MULTIPLE STREAMS AND SUSTAINABLE GROWTH

One of the biggest shifts in my journey to financial peace came with this realisation: relying on one income source isn't just limiting - it's stressful. No matter how well you budget or save, if your entire livelihood depends on a single paycheque, you're walking a tightrope. This understanding didn't come from fear, it came from a desire for *freedom*.

Though I had a stable government salary covering expenses and allowing for savings, I recognised that one policy change, leadership shift or health issue could easily disrupt that income. I didn't want to be at the mercy of external forces — I wanted options.

I began exploring multiple streams of income; not just more work for more money, but smarter systems for sustainable income. I looked inward, asking:

*What do I know that others want to learn?*
*How can I share my skills in ways that scale?*
*What value can I offer that doesn't depend on my physical presence?*

The answer became clear – financial literacy education.

I transformed my informal financial advice into a structured platform for Arabic financial education. I began designing workshops on budgeting, saving, and investing, launched online courses, and regularly shared content on Instagram and YouTube. The growth was far from instant. My first course took months to develop and attracted only a handful of sign-ups. My early videos barely got any views. But I stayed consistent and built trust; refining my message, learning what my audience truly needed. I focused on translating complex financial concepts into clear, accessible language that anyone could understand. Step by step, the platform grew - not just in numbers, but in impact.

Multiple income streams provide both financial security and psychological comfort. Knowing you're not dependent on any single source allows you to make decisions from strength rather than desperation. As I built these streams, I invested in learning every single day, pursuing certifications in several areas of finance and deepening my expertise. I transformed that growing knowledge into a company dedicated to financial education. The income I earned wasn't just spent, it was intentionally invested to generate passive income, allowing my money to work for me.

Building sustainable income streams requires long-term thinking. The focus should always be on creating consistent value rather than chasing quick wins. Everyone has expertise that others need - the key is packaging that knowledge in a way that genuinely serves your audience, while generating lasting income for yourself.

Ultimately, the goal of multiple income streams isn't to work more hours – it's to build systems that provide freedom and security, empowering you to live in alignment with your values and priorities.

## LEGACY AND LEADERSHIP – TEACHING THE NEXT GENERATION

One of my most sacred responsibilities, isn't just managing money for myself but teaching my children how to relate to it with confidence, intention and peace. Recognising how much of my own mindset was shaped by childhood experiences - the silence around money, the shame of saying 'I can't afford that,' the expectation to give without limits - I didn't want that legacy for my children.

I made an early decision that money would not be a taboo topic in our home. From a young age, I included my children in simple financial conversations. We discussed needs versus wants and created family savings jars. I gave them a small allowance, guiding them on what to do with the money: some for saving, some for spending, some for giving. I celebrated their choices and asked how they felt purchasing things with their own money. They glowed with pride.

These small moments were powerful, showing my children that money isn't scary or confusing, it's simply a tool they're capable of using well. As they grew, we talked more deeply. I shared my own mistakes, telling them about times I overspent, saved too late, or said 'yes' out of guilt. I let them see that financial empowerment is a journey, not a destination. It's about progress, not perfection.

Most importantly, I modeled what I wanted my children to learn. They saw me plan before spending, say 'no' to misaligned opportunities, budget joyfully rather than stressfully, teach others, and turn knowledge into income - all while giving, honoring both family and personal goals. As a result, money in our home never felt scarce, it felt intentional and abundant.

One touching moment came when my eldest said, 'Mama, I want to start my own investment plan so that my money grows.' That's when I knew the ripple effect was working - this wasn't just about my financial freedom, but theirs too. Children absorb our behaviors around money. If they see stress and disempowerment, that becomes their baseline. If they see calm, purpose awareness, and generosity, they inherit that peace. That's why I made it my mission to extend this beyond my home.

I began actively working with the Ministry of Education to integrate financial literacy into school curriculums, determined to give every child, not just my own, the tools to build financial confidence and freedom from a young age.

Teaching children about money is about wellbeing, agency and choice – not just about wealth. These skills serve them for life. Whether you're guiding a child or learning as an adult, the principles remain the same; awareness, intention and consistent action create lasting change.

By raising financially literate children and equipping others with these tools, we're not just transforming individual households, we're creating communities built on stability, empowerment and abundance.

## YOUR JOURNEY TO FINANCIAL PEACE BEGINS NOW

As I reflect on this journey from that broke twenty-year-old studying abroad to the woman I am today - financial educator, entrepreneur, mother and advocate - I'm struck by a profound truth: *you don't need to have everything figured out to begin.* You simply need a willingness to see clearly, feel honestly, and take one brave step towards peace.

Here are the five core messages from my journey that I hope will guide yours:

1. Transform Crisis into Catalyst: Your lowest financial moments often contain the seeds of your greatest growth. Instead of allowing shame to paralyse you, let it educate and motivate you towards better choices.
2. Build Independence Through Discipline: True financial freedom isn't about having vast wealth, it's about having the power to make life choices without money being the determining factor. This requires consistent, intentional habits that may feel restrictive initially but, ultimately, provide profound liberation.
3. Turn Personal Transformation into Service: Your individual journey can become a platform for helping others. The struggles you overcome and systems you develop often reveal exactly what the world needs you to contribute.
4. Create Security Through Smart Systems: Diversifying income streams and building a business aren't just about making more money, they're about creating options and peace of mind that allow you to live authentically and serve powerfully.
5. Build a Legacy of Empowerment: Financial peace isn't just personal – it's generational. By modelling healthy money habits and teaching financial literacy to children and communities, you create ripple effects that extend far beyond your own life.

To the person reading this – whether you're overwhelmed, generous to a fault, or unsure where your money goes, I want you to know that it's not a lack of intelligence or ambition. You simply need tools, clarity and permission to begin.

# BEGIN IT NOW

This is your permission slip.

You are not behind. You are not 'bad with money.' You are not too late.

You are someone who is ready. Ready to align your money with your values. Ready to breathe easier at night. Ready to build something lasting – not just in your bank account, but in your heart, your family and your future.

Start small. Track your spending. Define what peace looks like for you and plan, plan, plan. Examine your money beliefs. Create a simple budget reflecting your real life. Make one financial decision today that your future self will thank you for.

Financial freedom isn't reserved for a few, it's available to all who are willing to begin. You don't need perfection, higher income, or perfect timing. You need only to begin with what you have … where you are … today.

Close your eyes. Take a deep breath. Picture your most peaceful life – unburdened by shame, free from guilt, anchored in clarity. That life is possible.

The path to it begins with one step. It begins with you. It begins now.

# RANIA AL KHUSAIBI

Rania Al Khusaibi is the recipient of the *Women Who Change the World – Women in Finance* award (Bronze), honoring her exceptional efforts in transforming financial literacy across the Arab world. As the Founder of *Al Amal Consultancy* and the creator of the *Money by R*, Rania has become a leading voice in empowering individuals – especially women and youth— to take charge of their financial lives with purpose, clarity, and confidence.

A certified trainer and passionate financial educator, Rania has guided hundreds of individuals in breaking free from debt, building wealth, and making informed financial decisions. Her unique approach goes beyond numbers – blending emotional awareness, mindset shifts, and practical tools to help people reclaim control of their money and their futures.

Rania holds a Master's degree in Commerce from RMIT University in Melbourne, Australia, and a Master's in Leadership and Management from the University of Arizona's Thunderbird School of Global Management, completed in partnership with the Royal Academy of Management. She was selected among the top 1% of national applicants for this prestigious leadership program and completed it with distinction – while simultaneously running her business, managing her household, and raising three young children.

# RANIA AL KHUSAIBI

Throughout her career, Rania has contributed to several high-impact national programs aimed a more financially aware society in Oman. These initiatives, combined with her consultancy work, have given her deep insight into the financial needs of diverse communities, fueling her commitment to accessible and inclusive financial education.

Her signature workshop, *Her Wealth, Her Power*, guides women through a six-step roadmap to financial freedom, covering essential topics such as budgeting, saving, investing, and creating multiple streams of income to gain independence.

Rania has built a vibrant digital platform, her content viewed by over 100,000 viewers across Instagram, TikTok, and YouTube. Her Arabic-language content fills a critical gap in the financial education space, providing clear, culturally relevant, and engaging guidance for underserved audiences. Her work is changing the narrative around money – particularly for women – showing that financial independence is possible, practical, and deeply empowering.

In 2024, Rania was selected as a TEDx speaker, where she delivered a powerful talk on her personal journey with finance. Her message resonated widely, emphasizing that when individuals – especially women – understand and own their financial decisions, they unlock not just wealth, but confidence, dignity, and personal growth.

As a mother of three, Rania brings empathy and authenticity to everything she does. She understands the challenges of balancing family life with financial goals – and uses her own journey to inspire others to pursue a life of intention and abundance.

Website: moneybyr.com
Instagram: @money.by.r
YouTube: Money By R
Contact: rania@moneybyr.com

# THE HUMAN POWER
## THRIVING WITH EQ IN THE AGE OF AI

### ROMAA RAJADHYAKSHA

The rapid rise of artificial intelligence (AI) has reshaped the fabric of our world. Machines now process vast datasets at unprecedented speeds, algorithms predict patterns with remarkable accuracy, and automation drives global industries toward new horizons. While these technological feats are undeniably impressive, there is one domain where AI will never truly rival humanity: in the realm of emotional connection, empathy and intuition. These core human attributes, collectively known as emotional intelligence (EQ), define us in ways machines never can. As we move forward in an AI-powered future, it will be these profound human qualities that will continue to shape our world.

I remember a moment, a couple of years ago during a workshop I was running where a student, visibly nervous, struggled to share their ideas. Instead of pushing them to speak, I paused, acknowledged their feelings, and encouraged them gently. Minutes later, they opened up and shared an insight that shifted the entire discussion for the group. No algorithm could have recognised the tremble in their voice, the fear in their eyes, or known that what they needed most in that moment was empathy. It was a reminder that emotional intelligence is not abstract, rather it transforms real lives in real time.

The significance of emotional intelligence and soft skills, often referred to as power skills, is becoming more evident every day, not just in our personal lives but also in the professional world. As the landscape shifts towards more automation, our capacity for understanding, managing and connecting through emotions will set us apart in a world increasingly dominated by machines. I have seen this first-hand in corporate strategy rooms, where the most impactful leaders are not those with the flashiest presentations but those who listen deeply, read the room, and make every individual feel valued. It is the irreplaceable essence of being human – strengths like empathy, adaptability, leadership and emotional insight that will ultimately guide us to thrive amidst an evolving technological landscape.

## THE IMPRESSIVE RISE OF AI – AND ITS FUNDAMENTAL LIMITS

Artificial intelligence has exploded in recent years, transforming industries across the globe. AI can process vast amounts of data in an instant, predict trends, and automate complex tasks that once took humans hours, if not days, to complete. In medicine, AI assists doctors in diagnosing illnesses with remarkable accuracy. In business, it enables companies to forecast market shifts with precision. The power of AI seems boundless - and in many ways, it is.

However, for all its strength, AI has limitations. It can analyse patterns, predict outcomes, and even engage in basic decision-making, but it lacks the nuances of human interaction. AI cannot replicate the depth of emotion, the connection forged through empathy, or the ethical considerations that define our shared humanity.

For example, imagine a patient receiving a cancer diagnosis. A machine can analyse the patient's medical history and suggest the most effective treatment plan, based on data, but no machine can offer the comforting words of a doctor who listens, understands and reassures a patient through their fears. AI may have the facts, but it lacks the warmth that allows a person to feel truly supported.

This very limitation underlines the irreplaceable value of emotional intelligence. While AI excels in technical arenas, it is humanity's empathy and creativity that will continue to steer our most complex decisions.

**WHY EQ MATTERS MORE THAN EVER**
Power skills such as communication, emotional intelligence, resilience and leadership are no longer optional in the workplace; they are the currency of the future. As AI takes over repetitive tasks, what remains are roles that require strategic thinking, emotional insight and interpersonal dexterity.

Leaders who excel in emotional intelligence foster loyalty, inspire teams and navigate complex challenges with grace. Professionals who master effective communication stand out in negotiations, storytelling and influence. Those who cultivate adaptability remain indispensable in a world where change is the only constant.

Think of some of the most impactful figures in history - Mother Teresa, Nelson Mandela, Barack Obama, Jacinda Ardern. Their success is not built on technical skills alone but on their ability to connect, inspire and lead with emotional intelligence. Data may inform decisions, but it's emotional intelligence that sparks revolutions, heals hearts, and fuels human progress

At its core, emotional intelligence is the ability to recognise, understand and manage our own emotions, as well as the emotions of others. It encompasses a range of skills, including empathy, communication, self-awareness, adaptability and conflict resolution. These skills are what allow humans to navigate the complexities of relationships, to inspire others, and to solve problems in ways that machines simply cannot.

Take leadership, for example. In the corporate world, leaders with high EQ are the ones who create cohesive, high-performing teams. They know how to motivate their employees, resolve conflicts and build trust. These leaders don't just give orders, they understand the needs of their people and work with them to achieve a common goal. They recognise the importance of emotional connections in driving productivity and job satisfaction. When employees feel heard, valued and understood, they are more likely to be engaged and committed to their work.

In contrast, a leader who lacks EQ might struggle to connect with their team, leading to disengagement and low morale. They might make decisions based solely on data and efficiency, without considering the human impact. This is where emotional intellect becomes invaluable, helping individuals navigate not just the technical aspects of their roles, but also the interpersonal dynamics that define success.

## REAL-WORLD EXAMPLES: HOW EQ POWERS PERSONAL AND PROFESSIONAL SUCCESS

The role of emotional intelligence extends far beyond leadership in the workplace. Think of the countless everyday situations where EQ plays a pivotal role. Whether it's resolving a disagreement with a colleague, offering emotional support to a friend or managing stress during a challenging time, our ability to manage emotions and navigate social dynamics determines the quality of our relationships and our overall well-being.

In education, students with high EQ are often more successful than their peers. Emotional intelligence helps students manage the stress of exams, collaborate effectively with classmates and communicate their ideas clearly. A study published by the Collaborative for Academic, Social, and Emotional Learning (CASEL) found that students who received social-emotional learning (SEL) programs saw improvements, not only in their emotional intelligence, but also in academic performance.

No one is perfect, but let's take Jacinda Ardern as an example. As

Prime Minister of New Zealand during times of profound crisis - from the Christchurch mosque shootings to the global pandemic - she demonstrated a leadership style grounded in empathy, compassion and clear communication. She didn't just manage events, she held space for collective grief, fear and hope. Her ability to connect emotionally with both her citizens and the global community showed how deeply human-centred leadership can restore trust and inspire unity. AI may crunch numbers and deliver data-driven solutions, but it will never step in front of a microphone and say, with authentic conviction, 'They are us.' That kind of resonance and the ability to lead with both strength and softness is uniquely human.

## THE ROLE OF POWER SKILLS IN DECISION-MAKING AND PROBLEM-SOLVING

In decision-making and problem-solving, power skills like critical thinking, empathy, and adaptability are crucial. These skills allow individuals to consider not just data, but also the emotional and ethical implications of their choices, making them essential for responsible and effective decision-making.

For example, when a company faces a challenge such as implementing a cost-saving measure that might impact employee morale, critical thinking enables leaders to evaluate long-term effects, like disengagement or trust erosion, alongside financial outcomes. Empathy helps leaders understand the personal impact on employees, fostering decisions that balance profitability with human well-being.

In problem-solving, adaptability allows individuals to respond flexibly to evolving situations. Whether addressing a conflict in the workplace or finding creative solutions to complex issues, these power skills enable leaders to navigate ambiguity and identify solutions that might not be immediately obvious. Empathy fosters collaboration, ensuring that all perspectives are considered and valued.

While AI can analyse data and suggest solutions based on patterns, it lacks the human touch needed to assess emotions and navigate the nuances of relationships. Human problem-solvers, combining logic, emotional insight and creativity, can address challenges in a way that machines cannot, offering solutions that account for both the technical and human aspects of a situation.

## EMPOWERING THE NEXT GENERATION: DEVELOPING EQ & POWER SKILLS FOR ACADEMIC EXCELLENCE

Power skills such as emotional intelligence, communication and resilience are the bedrock of success - and not just academically, but in life. These skills go beyond the confines of traditional academic achievement and shape how individuals interact, solve problems and navigate life's challenges. Academic success isn't merely about grades, it's about the ability to manage stress, collaborate effectively and express oneself confidently.

The foundation for these skills begins early, with emotional intelligence having a profound and lasting impact. Children who develop self-awareness, understanding of their emotions and how they affect their actions ultimately tend to perform better academically and socially. Emotional intelligence equips students to manage stress, adapt to new situations, and build meaningful connections with peers. They approach learning with a sense of curiosity, and interpersonal relationships are marked by empathy rather than competition. These early developments lay the groundwork for emotional resilience, empowering students to tackle challenges with clarity and confidence.

Resilience and the ability to collaborate are essential qualities that contribute to long-term success. Students who develop resilience, who can rebound from setbacks and view challenges as opportunities for growth are more likely to persist in the face of adversity. Likewise, the ability to work well with others fosters teamwork and collaboration, skills that are indispensable in today's interconnected world.

Integrating social-emotional learning (SEL) into education ensures that students are equipped to handle both academic pressures and the complexities of social interactions. By prioritising the development of these power skills, we help students grow into well-rounded individuals, prepared for a future where emotional intelligence is as essential as intellectual ability. Ultimately, it's not just about grades, it's about grit. About grace under pressure. About growing into someone who doesn't just succeed … but helps others succeed too.

## OVERCOMING CHALLENGES IN DEVELOPING POWER SKILLS

While the importance of emotional intelligence and power skills is irrefutable, the journey to mastering these attributes is not always straightforward. Many of us grow up in environments where emotional expression is undervalued or misunderstood, leaving us ill-equipped to navigate the intricacies of our own emotions or those of others. Developing emotional intelligence requires self-awareness, vulnerability, and a willingness to engage deeply with both personal feelings and interpersonal dynamics - skills that are not always nurtured in traditional educational settings or societal norms.

The challenge lies not in the lack of potential but in the absence of focused guidance and support. In a world that often prioritises logic, efficiency and technical prowess, emotional skills are sometimes relegated to a secondary status, seen as *nice-to-haves* rather than essential components of success. This mindset has begun to shift, however, as more organisations, educators and thought leaders recognise the transformative power of emotional intelligence in fostering collaboration, innovation and leadership.

Moreover, societal pressures can sometimes hinder the development of these skills. Expectations to conform to rigid standards of behaviour or success often discourage individuals from embracing their emotional landscape fully. Yet, in the face of such challenges, there is an undeniable opportunity for growth. Building emotional intelligence requires intentional, conscious effort. It starts with a willingness to acknowledge that emotions are neither weaknesses nor distractions but integral parts of the human experience, that can drive creativity, connection and resilience.

Developing these power skills necessitates a commitment to lifelong learning, starting with the foundational practice of self-awareness. This journey involves becoming attuned to our own emotional states, recognising how our feelings influence our decisions and interactions, and cultivating an openness to feedback. Alongside self-awareness, empathy and active listening become essential tools. To truly connect with others, we must listen not only to their words but also to the unspoken emotions that shape their experiences.

Despite the inherent challenges, the rewards of developing emotional intelligence are profound. Those who master these skills possess an unparalleled ability to lead with authenticity, navigate conflicts with grace, and inspire others to reach their fullest potential. It's a continual process, but one that is vital not only for professional success but for creating a more empathetic and understanding world.

## THE FUTURE IS HUMAN: THE IRREPLACEABLE EDGE OF EMOTIONAL INTELLIGENCE

As artificial intelligence continues to evolve, it is easy to be captivated by its technological advancements and the immense potential it holds. AI is undeniably revolutionising industries, automating tasks, and processing vast amounts of data with unparalleled efficiency. Yet, amidst this wave of technological innovation, it is essential to remember what truly distinguishes us from machines - our humanity. The ability to connect, inspire and lead with emotional intelligence is not only what defines us, but it will be the cornerstone of success in the AI-driven future.

AI may excel in tasks that require data processing and automation, but it will never replicate the profound impact of human connection, creativity and empathy. These uniquely human traits are what allow us to navigate the complexities of relationships, solve problems with ingenuity, and lead with authenticity. As we transition into an era dominated by machines, those who can harness emotional intelligence will hold the competitive advantage. The future belongs to those who can thrive in the rich, nuanced spaces where AI cannot reach - spaces defined by emotional understanding and human connection.

The workforce of tomorrow will not be defined by speed or technical expertise alone. In a world where AI can automate the repetitive and predictable, the demand for critical thinking, persuasive communication, and empathetic leadership will grow exponentially. Companies are already shifting their focus. They no longer hire solely for technical prowess, but for those who can bridge the gap between AI's efficiency and the essential human impact. Professionals with high emotional intelligence, problem-solving abilities, and the skill to navigate ambiguity will be the ones who excel.

As we stand at the precipice of an AI-driven future, the question is not whether technology will shape the world - it already has. From algorithms that recommend the news we read, to online platforms that have redefined how we connect, work, and even learn, technology has rewired the rhythm of daily life in ways unimaginable only a generation ago. In healthcare, AI-powered systems detect cancers earlier than ever before, and wearable devices track our heart rates and sleep patterns, transforming how we understand and care for our health. Education, too, has been revolutionised: virtual classrooms connect students across continents, while personalised learning apps adapt to each child's pace and style. The true question is; *how will we shape our place within it?* To thrive in this new era, we must actively invest in developing the human skills that machines cannot replicate. The ability to listen deeply, to communicate with empathy, and to stay resilient in the face of uncertainty are not merely *nice-to-haves* but essential capabilities that will define success, both in the workplace and in life.

It's never too early to start cultivating these power skills. Whether in academic settings or professional environments, emotional intelligence will be the defining factor in future success. The human touch, the ability to connect and collaborate, will remain irreplaceable, no matter how sophisticated technology becomes. As we embrace the evolving landscape of AI, we must remember that what will always set us apart is not our ability to process data, but our capacity to connect, to understand and to lead with heart. As we shape this AI-powered world, let's not forget that our greatest competitive edge was never about being faster, it was about being *human*. And that is where the real future begins. So if you're wondering when to commence - start with yourself, and begin it now.

# ROMAA RAJADHYAKSHA

Romaa Rajadhyaksha is an empowerment coach, strategist, and an award-winning entrepreneur devoted to reimagining how we define success in a world shaped by speed, systems, and artificial intelligence.

As the founder of SWS Global Coaching aka StudyyWell Solutionss, she leads an education-first movement rooted in a powerful belief: emotional intelligence isn't a soft skill – it's a human one. Through immersive coaching, real-world workshops, and future-ready curriculum, she helps young people develop the power skills behind real success – resilience, stress management, self-awareness, empathy, and conflict resolution.

She also leads Strategic Growth Solutions Consulting, a boutique firm helping businesses craft bold, future-focused strategies – while integrating emotional intelligence and people-first leadership into their organisational DNA. Whether supporting startups, established enterprises, or emerging founders, her work sits at the intersection of strategic clarity and human insight.

With an academic background in Psychology and Criminology, and an MBA currently underway, Romaa blends academic insight with a lived understanding of what it means to lead with both head and heart. Her path has moved fluidly across corporate sectors – spanning boardrooms, grassroots education spaces, global youth forums, and United Nations platforms. In every space, she carries one guiding belief: the future won't be led by algorithms alone. It will be shaped by those who lead with purpose and intention.

Romaa is a Committee Member for the Commission on the Status of Women Australia (UN Women Australia), and the recipient of the Emerging Entrepreneur of the Year award at the Women Changing the World Global Awards 2025. Her work and thought leadership have been featured in feMENA Magazine, MSN (Microsoft), Insights Success and on global platforms focused on business, leadership, and education.

Romaa is also a co-author of *How to Survive and Thrive III,* alongside the Joe Foster, the founder of Reebok and a few other leaders and change makers globally.

What sets Romaa apart is not just what she builds – it's the energy she brings to it. With empathy as her compass and strategy as her craft, she meets people where they are, but never lets them stay small. Whether she's engaging with a global organisation, working with a young founder, or sitting across from a student with a dream, Romaa leads with compassion, strength, and something unmistakably human.

Her ultimate belief is: Success isn't about being the loudest in the room. It's about being the one who listens, who uplifts, who leads – with purpose and heart.

# BEFORE I FORGET

## SAODE SAVARY

## PROLOGUE

My career was booming with numerous contracts that demanded extensive travel and grueling 16-hour workdays, each filled with adrenaline and excitement. It was an exhilarating journey of learning and adapting to diverse organisational cultures and ever-changing business landscapes. This relentless pace left me with no free time for anything else. But when you called to inform me that ManmieNa was unwell, I took the first flight. Upon seeing her, I knew the end was near. A week later, you and I surrounded ManmieNa's bed, my sisters holding hands in prayer as she released her last breath.

Moments later, you asked to be left alone. Profoundly absorbed in your thoughts, you did not see me hiding, watching you, while waiting for the mortuary transporters to arrive; your eyes, two dark stars riveted on Mom's inert body. Your hands, limply clasped, supported your thumbs as they spun the wheel, each turn bringing back memories that wove through your life, but now crumpled the wrinkles, freeing the space for the silent tears that criss-crossed your melancholic face. I wanted to run and hug you, drying your tears, but I chose to respect your freedom to cry in dignity for your warrior worthy of a Marie-Jeanne Lamartinière[1]. ManmieNa had fought fearlessly in so many battles alongside you for 75

---
1 Marie-Jeanne Lamartinière: womensactivism.nyc/stories/9892

years, while raising a family of nine daughters and one son.

After her funeral, I decided to devote more time to you. You were happy for my decision. Together, we planned for month-long visits quarterly, while my sisters would rotate visits during the others. During these moments spent with you, we became like two old friends, remembering bygone family times, where you gave free rein to your nostalgia for the past. You were generous in sharing memories and commenting sharply on geopolitics. I was eager for advice, sharing my experiences in a professional world different from yours. I sometimes caught you challenging my memory (and testing yours) by asking me to recite your favorite poems: *"Après la Bataille."*[2] I deliberately made mistakes to give you the satisfaction of declaiming it triumphantly. With time, I watched you giving up slowly what was meaningful to you, moving away from life through slower steps, fewer words and longer naps. One day, you were surrounded by four of my sisters, when you drifted peacefully into your eternal sleep. Flying during COVID time was difficult, and to my great sadness, I landed on the day after you passed away. I was not there to hold your hands and close your eyes. You, so dear to me, are now gone, leaving me in deep grief. I am so grateful to have spent time with you when you needed it most. Reminiscing memories of our precious father-daughter talks fills me with gratitude for your unconditional love and unfailing support. Reflecting on these moments, I realised there were some questions left unanswered. I decided to begin writing the answers to you now … *Before I Forget…*

## NO, MADAM, I AM NOT A MAN

Do you remember how puzzled you were, when I told you that all along my career I have often been mistaken as a man because of my name? My

---

2 After the Battle/Après la bataille, poem by Victor Hugo poetica.fr/poeme-191/victor-hugo-apres-la-bataille/comment-page-2

first experience was in 1978 when I started as a chemist-in-training[3] at a chemical plant. The personal protective equipment (PPE) I needed to perform my job safely did not fit. When I returned it, the stockkeeping lady, perched on a ladder, shouted without looking at me:

*Sorry Sir, we do not have your size now!*
*Madam, I am not a man, I replied drily.*

She did not think it important to look at me, because her biased mindset was conditioned to assume that a *"new young chemist-in-training"* can only be a man. PPE was originally designed with anthropometric data of military men that defined standards for size and fit. Industries requiring the use of PPE were male-dominated.

The stockkeeping lady's perception aligned well with the operators I was supervising and whose welcoming words included: *"why did you decide to do a man's job?"* I spent several months explaining that no "man" ever had exclusive ownership over any profession. It took months for them to accept that a women chemist could deliver as efficiently as a man.

You once commented that, *'these people needed glasses to see."* Contrarily, I thought I faced an unconcealed systemic gender discrimination. The gender gaps in PPE fitness are directly related to the structural marginalization of women in the male-dominated science fields. Hence, in my view, *"these people"* needed to recognise their skewed systems that generate prejudices and gender stereotyping. When work environments became challenging, I decided not to include it in our daily phone conversations. It was tough learning to become a professional chemist while juggling with gender equality issues, structural barriers, racism, and at the same time, learning to become a working mum. I was steering solo

---

[3] Title conferred by the Ordre des Chimistes du Québec to professionals with less than 24 months of experience in the profession after graduating with a bachelor degree in chemistry or biochemistry. It takes 24 months of practical experience before earning the title of chemist. More at: ocq.qc.ca/profession/titres-professionnels

in the driver's seat, trying to find new directions without a co-pilot. My objective was to keep my position without risking my health. How I wished I had a mentor guiding me through professional role transitioning and integration! I heard you repeating: "*nothing to be frightened about, always something to understand.*" So, in challenging situations, I observe, understand, communicate, take action and grow. I stand for my rights, claim my place and my seat, and never hesitate to voice my opinion. I am not afraid of getting hurt or disturbing other people's comfort, and I remain open to learning and healing.

Then few months later, you asked: "*How did your lab coat story end?*"

I learned to "mend" the problem and tame the work environment. I started using custom – adjusted PPE and made sure everyone knew the situation was unacceptable. In searching for a solution, I embarked on a learning spree about health and safety regulations, workplace chemical hazard assessment, occupational exposure, fit testing, workmen compensation and workers protection, cross functional teamwork and structural inequalities. I collaborated with my supervisor, HR and procurement to introduce the need for women's sizes in PPE. However, the PPE industry was slow to follow, and systemic barriers continued to put women at risk and perpetuate gender inequalities. You will be surprised to know that today, women are still fighting to get adequate PPE to work safely[4].

This "*labcoat story*" shaped my career in Environment and Occupational Health and Safety. My Ph.D. research focused on integrated management systems in the high-risk Aluminium industry[5]. I authored a chapter in the first CIHR Casebook on the importance of

---

4 CSA Group (2022), Anya Keefe, Canadian Women's Experiences with Personal Protective Equipment in the Workplace, CSA Group, Standard Research availablecsagroup.org/wp-content/uploads/CSA-Group-Research-Canadian-Womens-Experiences-with-Personal-Protective-Equipment-in-the-Workplace.pdf?srsltid=AfmBOoo0sz8QJA-GT-NyBMBJmNA6bWOK8qPsWHHnUP0xmPB1qR-4hoVwq

5 Savary, Saôde (2009). Analyse d'implantation d'un système de gestion intégrée en environnement et en santé et sécurité du travail. Université de Montréal: umontreal.scholaris.ca/items/ff412906-a81d-4768-b39e-7a65a2de50b2

Gender in Research[6]. I mentored to Chemistry graduates transitioning to the workplace.

After years working in production, I decided to pursue a graduate degree, realising I had to enter the lion's mouth to reach my goal.

## THE DAY I ENTERED INTO THE LION'S MOUTH

During our conversation on strategies to overcome fear, you insisted to know what happened after I entered *into the lion's mouth*. The only evidence I have is that the beast did not eat me, otherwise I would not be there to tell you this story (that has not been told yet) – I am sharing with you ... *Before I forget*.

That day, I simply showed up for my interview and handed my convocation letter to the secretary. Her dismayed gaze remained fixed on mine as she held my letter in her trembling hands. Seconds of eternity preceded her jerky walk to the office door to announce, "Your appointment is here." Did I detect a nervous tremor in her shivering near-extinct voice as she repeated her sentence? Before I could assess, Dr. PA, the self-proclaimed "racist" whirled abruptly. His stupefied look, visibly alarmed, was flushed. It was a look of bewilderment and concern, welcoming a nasty surprise that heralded the return of a forgotten nightmare. While trying to gain his composure, he murmured with a rictus:

"So ... you are Savary?"

"Indeed, Sir. I am Saôde Savary," I replied.

In the deafening silence that filled the room, we were both immersed in our thoughts. Him, I suspect, was grappling with conflicting emotions, thinking that Black students, traumatised by his reputation, had systematically avoided his classes since after the "Computer Riots" - the

---

[6] Saôde, Savary (2012). L'influence du genre lors de l'implantation d'un système de gestion intégrée dans un environnement de travail industriel, in CIHR Institute of Gender and Health: What a difference Sex and Gender Make: A gender, sex and health research case book pp 60-68. Available at: cihr-irsc.gc.ca/f/documents/What_a_Difference_Sex_and_Gender_Make-fr.pdf

largest anti-Black racism student protest in Canadian History[7] in 1969. He, who at that time did, *"not apologize for being racist,"* must be wondering why I was there today?

I, unapologetic for who I am, was debating between the fearful threat of rejection and failure, anticipated by my friends who were victims of his racist darts, and the conviction that my grades entitled me rightfully to start this emerging interdisciplinary program only offered in that particular university in Canada. Suddenly, his forced-calm voice ruptured the silence:

"What can I do for you today?"

"I am here to discuss about my admission to the Ecotoxicology Graduate Program," I replied.

I remember the long conversation that ensued on organochlorine pesticides - both of us mutually aware of the fragility of the moment. This was followed by several conversations over the course of my study, where Dr. PA became very supportive of my achievements. In that fall 1985 cohort, I was the only black woman in the program.

When celebrating the 10th anniversary of the program, he begged for my presence. He waited for me to open the champagne and cut the cake. As he filled my glass, he thanked me for joining him. He opened his speech with this word, pointing at me with a happy smile: *"This lady, here, changed my life"* ... Only he knew what he meant. I had no time to decode his message, as my attention was riveted on the audience, sketched with a sizeable representation of black women and men among graduates and current students.

Leaving the ceremony, I kept thinking about the transformational outcome I witnessed. Cohorts of black and diverse students in a program led

---

[7] For more info: Sir George William Affair: en.wikipedia.org/wiki/Sir_George_Williams_affair
October 28, 2022- The Gazette: Concordia apologizes for its role in 1969 "computer riots," institutional racism: montrealgazette.com/news/article117140.html#storylink=cpy
Ninth Floor review: Documentary captures landmark moment in Canadian race relations By Bill Brownstein youtube.com/watch?v=iRNnTMIUe2A

by Dr. PA! Did I leave some slow-release healing pills in the lion's mouth? Fast forward to 2022, recommendations from the University President's Task Force on Anti-Black Racism included the legacy of the 1969 student protest in shaping institutional changes. This acknowledgement opened the door to healing for persons living with the post-traumatic sequela of that event.

To your question: *"What did you learn from this experience?"*

I remained authentic to my maverick self, giving Dr. PA opportunities to appreciate my abilities as a student and my values as a person, giving myself ample openness to understand how a racist mind operates, while learning not to become a racist myself. I learned to stay focused and grounded. I realised that past experiences are meant for learning and growth, and I should not let them determine my destination. I learned to be confident, brave and dare to jump barriers in order to progress in my journey.

## THE DAY I DECIDED TO BE MY OWN BOSS

After my son's birth, I re-entered the job market, confident that opportunities would flow, considering that graduates from my Ecotoxicology cohort were thriving in high-salary positions in Canada and abroad. I was disappointed that my intensive job search only led to bitter rejections. Regardless of other reasons, I was convinced these rejections reflected employers" blatant ignorance of market trends towards globalisation in a rapidly changing world, with lesser space for stereotype-makers. I decided then to become the architect of my career and told you of my decision to become my own boss. You sounded astonished when you asked: "When are you planning to start?" I replied enthusiastically, "I am ready to begin now!"

The time was right. The environmental awakening of the 70s had gained a world momentum. The prevalence of transboundary pollution has spurred the profusion of new regulations. Recommendations from Brundtland Report on Sustainable Development[8] ranged among top priorities in OECD countries. My academic background and experience were perfectly suited to meeting the needs of chemical companies in that global context. In 1989, I founded the Services d'Évaluation en Santé et Toxicologie Environnementale Inc., a consulting firm committed to helping SMEs[9] in the chemical sector manage their environmental and OHS[10] risks.

My major challenges were understanding the dynamics of entrepreneurship, finding resources, structuring my services and identifying a client niche. My self-employed status, with no active customer list denied me any chance to have a business credit line. I relied on the generosity of my bayby sister, Ingreed, for a loan that I reimbursed *"when things start getting better."* Today, women entrepreneurs, especially BIPOC women, continue to face challenges in terms of financing.[11]

I coached several environmental advocacy groups in developing evidence-informed arguments to support their presentations at the Office of Public Hearing on the Environment[12]. This experience provided me with a deep understanding of assessing the needs of local communities, communicating and collaborating with them. This became a useful asset in my consultant career and later.

In parallel, I earned certifications that allowed me to diversify my portfolio with new services on Phase I and II Environmental Assessment for Real Estate. I volunteered to write columns in Real Estate Newspapers. This resulted in successful access to an untapped client base in Canada and the USA. I contributed to public comments on standards and regulations

---

8 https://sustainabledevelopment.un.org/content/documents/5987our-common-future.pdf
9 Small and Medium size Enterprises
10 OHS: Occupational Health and Safety
11 Black Business and Professional Association (2021). Rise Up: A study of 700 Black women entrepreneurs: https://bbpa.org/wp-content/uploads/2021/04/bbpa-rise-up.pdf
12 https://www.bape.gouv.qc.ca/fr/

development by adding the ecotoxicological perspectives that were missing. I participated in numerous working groups, acted as a guest speaker, delivered professional workshops to diverse audiences. I have served on several boards of directors and participated in the development of criteria and skill sets that structured the accreditation of professionals in environment. I must emphasise that I was the only black woman among mainly professional men, who stayed loyal allies over the years. They helped me unlock many doors. Dr. PA, with whom I remained in close contact, recommended my service to my first big client. These networks provided me exposure to showcase my expertise, gain professional credibility and build reputational capital. As my career evolved from word of mouth in Europe and North America, I expanded my reach to high technology clients, contributing to the design and development of regulatory, Environmental and OHS risk management software, until I retire.

To hide my guilt as a travelling mum, I always dodged your recurrent question: "How are you managing with the kids?" Frankly Dad, I would confess today that it has been an uphill battle, with many lonely moments when I stood against the winds like a dignified Mangrove tree. I faced a constellation of aggressions, violences and abuses; rejections, pet to threat metamorphosis, credit thefts, client thefts, betrayals, competence sabotages, etc. I learned to map my own professional journey while navigating serenely between controversies, seeking understanding rather than consensus, ready to jump or shake barriers when unable to break them, and never giving up hope.

Being a consultant has been very hard work and long working hours. I had to keep up to date with knowledge in Environment and OHS, from the latest news, data, publications, technology, draft legislations and laws. I honored each contract with integrity, designing projects with uncompromised intellectual rigor that engaged every fibre of my brain, implementing evidence-informed solutions that improved management of risks in the workplace, pledging that workers will return home safely after their shifts, and committing that my clients will be among industry leaders with the best environmental and OHS practices.

I gained a wealth of rewarding experience that allowed me to unleash the immensity of my potential, go beyond my limits, grabbing opportunities that no workplace would ever offer me.

Today, Dad, I can tell you that I am proud to have pursued a career in science, against all odds. When no one would hire me, I had the courage to found and lead my own consulting firm while raising my children and earning two masters' degrees and a Ph.D. My children, now accomplished professionals, understand that my travels were part of the equation to make things work for the family and grow professionally. I feel blessed by their love and compassion, recognising that all this was possible because of your unconditional love, constant support and knowing that you and ManmieNa always had my back.

## THE DAY I DECIDED TO RETIRE

After ManmieNa passed away, I gradually retired to spend more time with you. During one of our conversations, you asked me:

"What would you change if you were to start over?"

I remember answering: "Make the world a better place with more humanity."

This was the embryonic vision that would drive my retirement project.

I joined the University Women's Club of Montreal (UWCM)[13] and was later nominated vice-president, then president. By the end of my term, I had successfully launched two flagship projects: Advocacy against Human Trafficking in collaboration with Free the Girls[14], and the Olympes de la Parole School Competition in collaboration with seven high schools in Montreal. Considering that social advocacy was not part

---

13 uwcm.com
14 freethegirls.org

of the UWCM's mission, the end of my mandate coincided with the conclusion of these projects. This is when I decided to create the Olympes de la Parole Canada / Voices of Olympia Canada[15] (ODPC /VOOC), a self-funded, volunteer-led, societal impact registered charity. It is named after Olympe de Gouges,[16] a French politician, playwright, early feminist and activist who authored *La Déclaration des droits de la femme et de la citoyenne* in 1791. Because of her writings, she was convicted of treason and was guillotined in Paris in 1793.

ODPC/VOOC is a scaling-deep project built with the vision of an intergenerational bridge leading to a world where girls are empowered to embrace the principles of global citizenship and become agents of change, contributing to the creation of a world where social justice and gender equality flourish. Our mission is to promote the voices of girls through four foundational pillars: Global citizenship - project-based learning, mentorship, promoting a culture of science, and meaningful youth community engagement. We cannot think of crafting a better world without early involvement of young girls in decision making process, for, they are the hope for the future and at the same time, the only future for hope.

The heartbeat of ODPC/VOOC is a yearly *juried* School Competition that offers high school girls in Canada a safe and informed discussion space to reflect on issues affecting women and girls, using a dual perspective of human rights and social justice. Our School Competition themes intersect with the sustainable development goals and issues discussed at the United Nations Commission on the Status of Women (UN-CSW). Our participants craft impactful youth-led projects in collaboration with local communities. This intentional collaboration helps them to recognise their common humanity and plant the seeds for solidarity, equality, compassionate leadership, respect, fairness and peace.

Participants submit their work to the selection jury, which adjudicates

---
15 olympesdelaparolecanada.ca/en/home
16 Olympes de Gouges: memoire-esclavage.org/biographies/olympe-de-gouges

the four best projects eligible for scholarships. The learning cycle culminates in participant's presentations at the Parallel Events Forum which links civil society to UN CSW. This event attracts an international audience of over 13,000 annually. For the past four consecutive years, ODPC/VOOC has coached 38 presentations on this platform.

Besides self-reported positive impact on participants, teachers and parents, our school competition indirectly impacts more than 75,000 students among the 24 participating schools across Canada. Over the years, ODPC /VOOC has established deep connections with both Indigenous and non-Indigenous communities, developed strong partnerships with international, national and local organisations, and served as an incubator for 42 high-impact projects.

Olympes de la Parole Canada is more than a program—it is a movement of hope, a testament to the boundless potential of girls rising together to transform their communities and our world.

And this is where I landed, Dad … when you left us.

## EPILOGUE

Dad, As I traveled my journey, I discovered humanity in its splendour and its ugliness. I continue to believe we can work together with the youth to make the world a better place, by refusing to normalise injustice and inequalities, and by accepting that we are all different and yet connected in the same world.

When a door closes, I keep knocking on others, knowing there are allies waiting to hold my hands and help me make the next move. A closed door remains much less important in my journey than an open door.

When I encountered bigotry and institutional barriers, I uprooted them, shook them away, or simply jumped over them, staying focussed on my destination, refusing to let my compass be calibrated by the values

# BEGIN IT NOW

or the manipulations of others.

When I faced violence and abuse, I denounced them loudly and promise never to be complicit in them. I spread compassion, protected myself and made allies.

The most difficult moment in my journey was when I had to leave my children. The night before a flight, we usually had family time where my daughter would sing *"You are my sunshine,"*[17] followed by my son, *'Ain't no sunshine when she''s gone…"*[18] As the plane took off, I could still hear their little voices competing with the roar of the engine, reiterating their love, and confiding their sadness and worry. Only then, did I allow myself to release the tears I had been suppressing.

As I reflect on my journey, I am filled with gratitude for the lessons learned and the endurance built. I am forever indebted to those who trusted my competence and were not afraid to open their doors, allowing me to enter and collaborate with professionalism, respect, open mindedness and fairness.

To those who erected barriers, I simply say: *the higher your barriers, the further I will go.* In my consultant's world, there are no glass ceilings, there are only barriers to jump or break. My ceiling was the open sky, and my skyline was the sea. I traveled my journey, standing on the shoulders of those who came before me. I was fully aware that each step I took was blazing a trail for other women. I felt a responsibility towards humanity to make this path accessible so that future generations could move forward with fewer obstacles, holding each other's hands to form a horizontal chain of solidarity, so greatly needed by humanity.

Dad, I welcome this unique opportunity to answer some of your questions now. I am more grateful than you'll ever know for your unwavering love, support and wisdom that have been my guiding light through

---

[17] You are my sunshine: en.wikipedia.org/wiki/You_Are_My_Sunshine, youtube.com/watch?v=5TUzB2fBUpY
[18] Bill Wihers – Ain't No Sunshine: youtube.com/watch?v=hPOYc4a2RPY

uncertain times. Thank you for always believing in me and encouraging me not to be afraid to dare. Your words and love have been my strength; ManmieNa's courage has been my inspiration.

Keeping you close in my heart with filial love,
Saôde

# SAODE SAVARY

Saôde is a chemist specialized in Environment, Occupational Health and Safety. Her career as an international consultant spans over 30 years supporting chemical industries solve complex international regulatory compliance and chemical risks challenges. Leading cross functional teams in different geographic settings in North America and Europe, she delivered landmark solutions in systems auditing, accreditation preparedness and compliance, chemical and toxicological data architecture, Life Cycle assessment and product stewardship, occupational risk management, regulatory content management and EHS software development.

Saôde is a retired member of l'Ordre des Chimistes du Québec where she chaired for several years the Environment sector and led the structuration of Chemistry students' chapters in several universities. Board Member of various professional associations, she is known for early involvement in taskforces that pioneered the development of the first accreditation criteria to certify Professional Environmental Auditors, as well as the development of the first National Skill - Set and criteria to certify Environmental Specialists in Canada. She was also a member of the Canadian Evaluation Society Sub Committee on Professional Designation criteria project. She reviewed and authored book chapters and contributed to several professional online communities of practice.

She holds a Ph. D. in Public Health from Université de Montreal School of Medicine, a master in Environment from Université de Sherbrooke, a graduate Diploma in Ecotoxicology and a Bachelor degree in Science from Concordia University.

Parallel to her professional career, Saôde is a Human Rights and Social Justice advocate. Her involvement in Canada's Treasury Board Secretariat's Employment Equity Committee earned her the Employment Equity Award in 1997. She dedicated her retirement in promoting girls' leadership and a culture of science since 2015. She conducted landmark awareness and educative work in several schools on the prevention of Human Trafficking. In 2017, she launched the first Olympes de la Parole School Competition in North America, and the sixth worldwide. In 2019, she was designated a «Notable Women» by the Canadian Federation of University Women. In 2023, she was honoured with the "Women of Distinction Award" by the YWCA de Montréal; that same year she was nominated a "Women of Distinction" by the Quebec Orientation and Work Integration Service for Immigrants (SOIT). In 2024, she was in nomination for the Exceptional Woman of Peace Award. In 2025, she became a finalist of the Women Changing the World Award in 2 categories: Human Right and Youth Impact.

# BEGINNINGS IN CHAOS

## SARAH MACRAE

Life has a way of throwing you into the deep end … without checking if you can swim. For me, that moment came weeks before my eighteenth birthday.

Living in a small country town, I was chasing a future I thought I could control. I had an apprenticeship as a chef; my hands always smelling faintly of garlic and herbs, my mind filled with dreams of kitchens and creation. I believed the world was a place of opportunity - innocent, even. That illusion shattered in a way I'll never forget.

I was robbed. It wasn't just the theft of my belongings, it was the theft of my sense of safety; the quiet certainty I'd carried about *the way the world worked*. The attack left me with a double fracture in my right elbow and upper shoulder, broken ribs and a fresh, searing awareness that life could turn without warning.

I woke in a hospital bed, battered but conscious. When a social worker came to sit beside me, she told me they'd run routine tests before deciding on surgery for my fractured arm. One of those tests changed my life forever.

'You're pregnant.'

The words felt as if they echoed in the air between us, floating there while I tried to process them. I wasn't ready. Not for this. Not for the world as it had just revealed itself to be. And yet, ready or not, life had decided my path was going to change.

## THE BEST AND SCARIEST THING

My first daughter arrived, and with her came a tidal wave of emotions. It was the best thing I had ever done - and God, it was terrifying. She cried, I cried. I thought it would all come naturally, like the world had promised in soft-focus magazine spreads and fleeting glimpses of other mothers. But it didn't.

Some things clicked instantly. Others … well, they took time. They took grit. They took the kind of patience you don't know you have until you're standing in the middle of the night with a screaming baby, wondering how *you got here* and whether you're doing anything right.

That's the thing about beginnings. They're messy. They're imperfect. And if you wait for the day when all your ducks are neatly in a row, you might never start at all. I could have backed away, played it safe, told myself I wasn't ready. But beginnings don't wait for readiness. They demand courage … and they often demand it before you even know you have any.

## THE YEARS OF GRIT

The years that followed were a mix of survival and building. I worked jobs, any jobs, to make ends meet. Hospitality, retail, shifts that started before sunrise and ended long after the rest of the world had gone home.

At the time, it felt like I was just hustling to keep the lights on and the fridge full. But what I didn't realise then, was that I was building a skill set. Every job, every challenge, every moment where I had to adapt and think outside the box, was quietly shaping me into the person I would need to be.

Those years taught me how to problem-solve on the fly, how to connect with people from all walks of life, how to read a room and see the gaps nobody else noticed. They were lessons I couldn't have learned in a classroom – and they were the foundation for something much bigger.

## A NEW CHAPTER – TWICE OVER

Just when I thought life had already given me its biggest plot twist, my second daughter arrived. And wow … what a force she was from the start.

Her birth was not an easy entrance into the world. She came early, tiny and fragile; weighing not even two kilograms. The doctors used the words *growth restricted*, but I saw nothing but a fighter. She was fierce like her sister before her. Holding her in my arms, I felt our little family was complete - just me and my two girls against the world.

Ironically, life decided to throw in another challenge. Not long after she was born, I fell down a flight of stairs while carrying her. I somehow shielded her, but the accident left me with ruptured discs in my neck. The physical pain was intense … but the thought of what could have happened to her was far worse.

As the years unfolded, our *little firecracker* began showing the same determination she had the day she was born. She hit her own milestones in her own way, with a spark that was impossible to ignore. Eventually, we learned she was on the autism spectrum and also had ADHD. Those labels didn't define her, they just explained her extraordinary way of seeing the world.

But those years opened my eyes in a whole new way. I began to see the cracks and failures in the systems around us; schools that put her in the 'too hard' basket, bureaucracies that seemed designed to exclude anyone who didn't fit into a perfectly round hole.

There were long stretches when she was at home with me - days, weeks, even months -because the educational system simply didn't know what to do with a child like her. And as much as those moments were heavy, they were also the moments where my resolve hardened.

Because in between supporting her and navigating endless meetings, I was also building a business. What began as a vision for people with disabilities now had a new, personal fire behind it. She wasn't just my daughter, she became a living reminder of why change was non-negotiable.

Sixteen years separated my first-born and my second, but together they became my reason to take life by the horns. We would fight the red tape. We would challenge the 'one-size-fits-all' mentality. And we would create spaces where no one ever felt they didn't belong.

She became our newest spark; the one who reminded us that beginnings happen over and over, and every new challenge is a chance to make a game-changing move.

## THE BUSINESS THAT BROKE THE MOULD

The business grew. Not because I had all the answers, but because I refused to accept the wrong ones. Every time someone told me, 'That's just how the system works,' I thought, *Well, then the system needs to change.*

I designed services and programs for people with disabilities that didn't just fit within the usual frameworks, they broke them. We looked at what people actually needed, not just what funding packages said they could have. We thought outside the box, and then outside of that box too.

I didn't want to just create a service, I wanted to create a movement. A place where people could grow, where they could rise from whatever ashes life had left them with, and see their own beauty reflected back at them.

We became a recognised name; internationally, nationally, and most importantly, in our own community. Our open doors were an invitation to take up space, to be loud, to be proud, to lead.

## THE PHOENIX TRIBE – RISING FOR ALL OF US

By the time the business was thriving, it was more than a workplace – it was a living, breathing community. We became known as the Phoenix Tribe … and we wore that name with pride.

Here, people didn't just belong - they created. They built their own beginnings. They chased their dreams. They rose, stronger each time, knowing they had a tribe behind them.

And right at the heart of this transformation was my second daughter. Her challenges, her brilliance, her relentless spirit – they had become part of our DNA. She reminded us daily that the systems we were fighting weren't abstract … they were personal. She was the face of every child who had been told they didn't fit in. The voice for every family worn down by bureaucracy. The fire that lit our determination to keep going when it would have been easier to stop.

The Phoenix Tribe wasn't just my vision anymore, it was hers, too. Her resilience had shaped our resilience. Her battles had sharpened our purpose. And her victories, big and small, had shown our entire community what it looked like to rise, again and again, no matter how many times the world tried to clip your wings.

Because beginnings aren't just a moment in time. They're a choice we make every day. And in our tribe, we don't just survive – we rise. Together.

# SARAH MACRAE

Hi, I would like to introduce myself. My name is Sarah MacRae, the eldest of four siblings, born and raised amidst the picturesque freezing landscapes of the Southern Highlands. My journey has been one of resilience and transformation, despite facing personal tragedy, such as the loss of my youngest brother, Keith. Throughout these challenges, I've achieved milestones that I am genuinely honoured to share.

I'm a proud mother to two amazing girls, Emily-May and Macie, who are the center of my universe. My greatest achievements are undoubtedly my children, and I am deeply grateful for the unwavering love and support from my incredible partner, Rael. Rekindling our high school romance 25 years later, Rael has been my soulmate and my strength. My family and close-knit tribe mean everything to me, especially my youngest daughter, who, at just eight years old, faces challenges with ASD and complex trauma. Her resilience is awe-inspiring and motivates me to keep going through life's ups and downs.

Balancing motherhood and running my own business isn't easy, but it's a challenge I embrace with grace and courage. My dedication to my daughters' well-being drives me forward, pushing me to overcome obstacles and seize every moment.

# SARAH MACRAE

28 years of experience in the disability field, advocacy is in my blood. It's a privilege to speak up for those who often don't have a voice of their own. I am on a mission to raise awareness and promote inclusivity. Everyone deserves to be valued and empowered, regardless of their abilities.

I have a relentless drive that stems from transforming my emotions of anger and hurt into a powerful force for creating and achieving. societal change or nurturing my daughters' growth, I give it my all. Each day is an opportunity to make a positive impact.

In my story, you'll find a blend of resilience, compassion, and determination. I'm here to leave my mark, to inspire others to embrace their journey, and to make a difference in the world. With every step I take, I'm reminded that the greatest achievements often come from the toughest challenges.

Beyond my roles as a mother and advocate, I've had the privilege of being involved in various community initiatives. giving back to the community is a core value I hold dear. I've seen firsthand the power of collective action and its positive impact on the world around us

Looking ahead, I'm excited to continue my journey of growth and impact. Whether expanding, growing my business, or simply being there for my family, I'm committed to making the most of every opportunity. As I navigate the road ahead, I'm grateful for the love and support of those who have been by my side every step of the way.

With love in my heart and fire in my soul, I'm ready to take on whatever challenges lie ahead continuing making a positive impact in the lives of others.

Website: 247careservices.com.au

# WHO I WAS MEANT TO BE

## SHARON SWIETEK

Have you ever held a secret so big it threatened to consume you? Or have you lived through an overwhelming experience that caused you to later wonder whether it was real or imagined?

If so ... I can relate.

Trauma does not discriminate. It can happen to anyone, at any time, when the nervous system is overwhelmed to the point it cannot process the experience, be it from a singular event, such as a near death experience or natural disaster, or consistent exposure to significant emotional distress, like chronic emotional neglect or physical abuse. No two people experience trauma the same and its effects are often long-lasting and devasting to the individual. However, healing is possible - no matter how distant it may seem or at what age you begin. For years, I carried the secret of my childhood sexual abuse, alone, and often questioned its reality. My healing journey began with the dawning light of comprehension and led to eventual recovery. It was not easy nor was the road straight. I suffered setbacks amongst the breakthroughs and endured a wild ride on an emotional rollercoaster - but eventually I found peace. Through my story, I hope to show you that, regardless of the source of your trauma, it's possible to live in the light again, even if all you can see is the dark right now.

I was four years old when I first experienced sexual abuse. I had begged my parents to allow me to sleep over at a neighbor's house. My only recollections are vague memories of a man approaching me as I woke from sleep, lying stiff as a board for the rest of the night on the floor that was my sleeping space, and fleeing for home at first light. Yet, despite the lack of specifics, I always had a nagging sense that something untoward happened to me. I suffered a recurrent nightmare for years after, and to this day, I have a deep-seated fear response if anything is placed directly in front of my face.

By the time I was eight years old, I found myself in multiple other uncomfortable situations. On several occasions, my brother's friend, who was 12 years old, coerced me into 'playing doctor.' For a long time, I felt ashamed and believed I had no right to call myself a victim – first, because my abuser was a child; and second; because I went along with it. Additionally, the adult son of family friends exposed himself to me. I thought I egged him on, and therefore, his action was my fault. Time and time again, doubts swirled in mind – *was I actually abused?* The fact that my earliest memories were cloudy at best and my belief that I had voluntarily participated in the other acts kept me from telling anyone what happened. The secret ate away at my self-worth and confidence, bit by bit, like a tidal surge eroding a sandcastle.

My family later moved several states away and in my child's mind, I thought, *I've left it all behind.* However, several years later, my parents announced that their friends and adult son would be visiting for a day as they passed through the state. I was immediately petrified … and frozen. I thought of telling my parents why I was scared, but that would mean revealing what I did to cause the behaviour. When the day of the visit came, I retreated to my room. Unfortunately, the son followed me, telling the adults he'd play with me. He suggested a game of hangman. I hesitated, but because I was a lonely child and part of me was excited that someone wanted to spend time with me, I agreed … despite my trepidation. He tried to engage me in conversation about what had previously occurred. I played dumb and I quickly solved the game. To my horror, the answer was the act he had done before. I fled to the safety of my mother's side, but my brain wouldn't stop thinking about what had just happened. *Why did he bring up what had happened years before?* Did I give him some indication I was amenable to his advances? I had no answers. Only questions.

I distinctly remember being alone with my mother on our basement stairs, later that day. I couldn't keep it inside anymore. The constant questioning of myself and turmoil of emotions inside made me feel as if I was about to burst. Gathering my courage, I quickly told her about the hangman game. My mother responded, He was probably just trying to see how far he could get. *Just stay away from him for the rest of the day.* That was it. No outrage. No voiced concern. No confronting him or any other protective measure. To say I was shocked is an understatement. I was eleven years old and he was twenty-three! I thought she would validate my feelings, reassure me that his actions were inappropriate, but instead she dismissed them and acted like it wasn't a big deal. *Was she saying this behaviour was normal or that I shouldn't be concerned?* I was so confused. I'd been prepared to tell her everything, about each indecent thing done to me in my short life, but her response left me feeling hollow and unseen. In that moment, I didn't know if telling her more would matter, should matter … so I stayed silent.

Two years later, another move, another state. I tried to simply forget about all the unpleasantness. I gathered up all those memories and feelings and shoved them into a dusty corner of my mind. However, when I was fourteen years old, it all resurfaced when the father of the child I was babysitting propositioned me for oral sex. When I declined, he exposed himself to me to show me what I was missing. I froze, then fled the house, not bothering to get paid. I distinctly remember walking down the driveway asking, 'Why me … again?' Did I have a bullseye or neon sign on my forehead that predators could see? *Could he tell this had happened to me before?*

I was so distraught over the fact I had been targeted once again. Was I wrong to feel I had been repeatedly abused? A firestorm raged within me and I wanted answers. But who would listen, really hear me? The experience with my mother years earlier meant I didn't feel I could talk to her and going to my dad was out of the question, due to our contentious relationship at the time. I decided to broach the subject with my grandmother who lived with my family. I didn't tell her about what happened that day, instead shared, without details, that I thought I'd been previously abused. I had no idea that she would tell my parents. However, later that night, my father called me to the living room and confronted me. I was interrogated. What happened? By Whom? When? Why hadn't I told him? He was upset and so very angry. *I felt his anger was directed solely at me.* I believed I had failed because I did not tell when I should have. His anger made me feel that the abuse was my fault, even though it was never explicitly stated. It seemed nothing good ever came from revealing my trauma.

During college, I tutored domestic violence survivors and worked in the rape unit of a prosecutor's office. I was drawn to this work, and felt an affinity with these survivors, yet still questioned whether I deserved to say I had a place in their ranks. I felt like a fraud. *I could not remember* the first incident, the second *involved another child*, and the other times I *wasn't physically touched*. But every time someone shared a personal story of abuse, every time I read a news article about a rape that occurred, a feeling of kinship stirred within me. During my senior year, I reached a breaking point. Once again, the emotions I had pushed down for years threatened to explode. With a deep breath and a prayer, I decided to seek professional help and dared to hope that I might find answers. A visit to my college counselor allowed me to see clearly. I had indeed been abused ... many times. It was the first time I felt truly heard and seen. She listened without judgment, spoke calmly and accepted what I told her at face value. She confirmed what I knew in my heart and permitted me to consider myself a victim. It was the moment I began healing.

In my early twenties, I started therapy with a psychologist who had worked with trauma survivors. Despite being in and out of therapy during my teens, none of those therapists had been trauma-informed and only sought to deal with the immediate problems in my life. They could not see that the root of my issues lay much deeper. My new psychologist understood my daily struggles with depression and emotional regulation were actually effects from my trauma. As I laid bare my past experiences and spoke openly about them, they began to be real to me in a way they never had before. Being able to frame them in the context of abuse settled the whirlwind of uncertainty that had plagued me for years. The trauma effects did not disappear, but at last I was able to make sense of it and thus find peace with what had happened. I learned that loss of memory does not mean the trauma did not occur. Child on child sexual interaction, where there is a disparate age and knowledge base, is abuse. A child cannot consent - no matter what - regardless of willing participation. Physical touch is not a necessary component of sexual assault. And the coat of shame was never mine to carry, but rather, belongs solely on my abusers. These were key understandings for my healing.

Trauma is not something that merely happens to us. It embeds itself in every cell of our being. Memories are not just stored in our brain. This explains my visceral belief that I was abused when I was four years old. Even though I cannot recall the specifics, my body remembers. In order to heal, we must learn to trust ourselves – trust our feelings and embrace them. Additionally, we must face our trauma. Pretending it didn't happen is not a solution. Compartmentalisation does not contain our trauma. It finds a way out, seeping through the edges of that imaginary box in your mind no matter how tight you think the box is sealed, influencing our reactions and behavior. My trauma deeply affected my ability to connect with others and make friends. I was extremely sensitive to criticism and viewed friendly gestures with suspicion. In essence, I felt my world wasn't safe. This manifested in low self-esteem and isolation from my peers. Moreover, hiding from trauma or not recognising it, leaves you vulnerable to revictimisation. Looking back, I'm not surprised that I was abused time and again. Predators are highly adept at seeing a child's vulnerabilities. My self-loathing was apparent in the way I carried myself. A few probing questions and my lack of social support was revealed. I ticked all the boxes.

As a part of my healing, I began researching and reading about sexual abuse and the trauma inflicted as a result. There was comfort in knowing others had similar experiences. Sexual abuse survivors are often not believed, dismissed, or told to 'keep quiet and endure.' It is why so many survivors never disclose. I thought that if I could help one person be heard and understood, my struggles would have been worth it. I began by speaking more candidly with friends about the topic and was surprised by the number of people who quietly reached out to share their stories. I shared mine in turn, showing them concretely with a tangible example in front of them, that I understood their pain and they were not alone. Later, I began working with more trauma survivors through a local organisation. Each time I told my story, I felt stronger and imbued with more agency over this aspect of my life. Furthermore, speaking my truth and helping other survivors had exponential healing power - within myself and the others I touched.

Healing from my trauma also meant facing past hurts and reconciling my feelings towards my parents. For years after my disclosures, I was angry with my mother and deeply hurt by my father's response. I understand now that neither had the tools necessary to support a survivor. For my mother, it was easier to downplay the incident than it was to acknowledge it. Looking at my father's reaction now, I see that his anger was over that fact I endured abuse from which he could not protect me and his rage was directed at the abusers who would not face justice due to the applicable statute of limitations. With what they know now, both would have handled my disclosure differently. To properly support survivors, it is critical that they are heard, seen and have a safe, non-judgmental environment to navigate through the complex web that is trauma recovery. However, healing from trauma is never linear. It can be messy and sometimes chaotic. My progress has been derailed time and time again. There have been triggering events that have sent me into temporary spirals, and others that have resulted in years-long depressive states where all I could do was the bare minimum to survive. However, knowledge is power, and the more I've learned about trauma and its effects, the better I've been able to cope with these setbacks and begin healing again. There are a wide range of therapies that have helped me, such as journaling, breathing exercises, yoga, meditation, and expressing gratitude for three things each day. I've learned to give myself grace when negative thoughts want to overwhelm me. I acknowledge these thoughts, let them pass through and replace them with self-affirmations. Practicing mindfulness, body-based therapies such as tapping acupressure points, singing, dancing, art, and physical exercise, as well as grounding techniques, are additional tools in my toolbox of positive coping skills. No one tool is best. And the tool I need for a particular challenging circumstance may not be the same one that worked before. But with all of them at my disposal, I feel more confident each day that the toughest part of my healing journey is behind me. I have moved from merely existing to actually living.

Now is my time to thrive. I'm following my passion and purpose, finding significant fulfillment in helping other trauma survivors. It is the reason I began my online peer support platform, where trauma survivors can connect with one another and build community. I am not a licensed mental health professional. I hold no pertinent degrees. I have merely walked the same path and hold space for those who need empathy, compassion and understanding. Trauma can be isolating for many survivors. Connection is a balm on our wounds. When survivors have their reality validated by others and witness healing is achievable, they are freed from viewing their circumstances as an inevitability.

But healing from trauma begins with a choice. A choice to prioritise yourself and do the work necessary to release the trauma. The path to betterment is not easy. But it is possible. If you are ready to heal, choose to begin it now. You will never be the same, but that does not mean 'less than' your former self. You survived and *can* thrive. Trauma survivors are the strongest people I know. We suffered. We endured. And yet we still stand. If you have endured any form of trauma, I see you, I hear you and I believe you. You are not alone.

# SHARON SWIETEK

Sharon Swietek is an award-winning trauma educator and attorney, having worked with trauma survivors in her personal and professional capacity for over 30 years. She is also the creator of Surviving Together, a YouTube channel, which is a safe space for trauma survivors to connect and build community on their healing journeys, as well as provides trauma-related education to survivors and non-survivors alike. Her work in the trauma field was recognized by Women Changing the World Global Awards when chosen as the 2025 winner in the Women in Journalism and Media category. As a survivor herself, Sharon is passionate about helping survivors see their true potential and dedicated to spreading mental health awareness to reduce the stigma of trauma.

# THE POWER OF FOLLOWING YOUR HEART & STARTING OVER

### SINJA HALLAM

*Yesterday I was clever, so I wanted to change the world. Today I am wise, so I am changing myself.*
– Rumi

There's something poetic, and a little ironic, about being asked to write a chapter in a book called *Begin It Now* … because beginning is not something I did once, it's something I've had to find the courage to do again and again. Most times, with the ground shaking beneath me. Sometimes willingly. Never with a plan neatly in hand.

I struggle with it. Why? Because beginning has rarely been convenient, glamorous or clear for me. But when I rifle through my memory bank as I write, I realise it has always been powerful. Every. Single. Time.

I didn't always know what would come next. My heart knew, though, that I couldn't stay where I was. As I chose my next steps, however tender and unsure they were, the path would always begin to appear beneath my feet.

This is why I've shared my favourite quote above with you. It's a reminder that before you can change the world, you need to change yourself - something I wish, more than anything, people in leadership positions would recognise. It would make our organisations places in which we can all thrive and not places we have to survive. Transformation begins with you. In you. Not outside of you. I have irrefutable evidence that everyone can do it. The difference between those who do and those who don't … is courage and deciding.

There are many stories of personal change, transformation and reinvention that I could tell:

When I upended my life and moved countries … not once but three times.

When I was cheated on by my first husband six months after we got married, then got divorced, and I had to begin in a new country with no support, no friends, and no job … I literally had nothing.

When I was made redundant four times in my career, and each time I had to reinvent myself to go further than I had before.

Or the time when I burned out.

That last one sounds like it should have been the easiest to manage, but it was the hardest. Here's why.

About 18 months after having upended my family's life to move from Adelaide, Australia, to Auckland, New Zealand, for a career opportunity, I found myself sitting bolt upright in bed.

I remember it clearly. It was a rainy Monday morning in Auckland. I was drenched in sweat, my heart racing and thoughts spiraling. Yet again.

What I didn't know in that moment, was that what was about to happen to me that day, would set in motion events that would change my life in unimaginable ways.

The familiar pit in my stomach began to form. My limbs felt like lead. My body was begging me to stay in bed. Then came the dread; heavy, as I dragged my weary bones to the bathroom. The dread of having to go to work and face what I knew was waiting for me.

To the outsider, I had it all. An amazing, supportive husband; who is and always has been my rock and the wind beneath my wings. A son, who knows and sees me - and who I am immensely proud of. A fabulous home. A well-paying job. And even at my age, a promising career trajectory.

But on the inside? A totally different reality. I felt unfulfilled. Lonely. Numb. Like I was missing something or missing out entirely. I wanted more and then felt immediately guilty, greedy, and ungrateful for even thinking that.

Like most women do, I pushed through the unease. I looked at myself in the mirror and whispered; *You can do this, Sinja. It will be ok. You've got this.*

On the bus to work, I leaned my head against the window. My eyes followed the raindrops trickling down, making squiggly little lines I traced with my finger. A quiet voice popped into my head and asked; *When was the last time you felt alive? Where did your joy go? Who even are you right now ... and where are you going?*

I had no answers.

What I did know was that I didn't recognise myself. I was never the type of person who *wasn't* joyful or didn't know how to cope, even when things got stressful or felt out of control. I was used to doing hard things. I had proof that I could, but right there, in that moment, on that uncomfortable bus seat, I felt like my heart and soul had shriveled up.

Just like the raindrops on the glass, tears started to trickle down my face, as I remembered what my husband and son asked me at the breakfast table that morning:

'Why are you so angry most of the time?'

I defended myself. I didn't think I was angry. But now, upon reflection, I realise my reaction told the truth.

I hadn't noticed how the smallest mishaps were triggering big, angry, defensive reactions from me. There were many. Beneath the surface, a storm was brewing. A bottled-up rage I didn't know how to explain. If I was totally honest with myself, that rage had been a constant companion for some time now.

That gentle voice came back again; *What are you going to do? You know you can't stay like this. Something has to change.*

I was too exhausted to think, let alone change anything. I just wanted to get through my day.

My work was orchestrating change and transformation at scale. Supporting others through it; through their resistance, their breakdowns, and their breakthroughs. The pace of change was relentless. And when it came to looking at my own? I brushed that inner nudge aside like it was dust on my coat. *Not now. I don't have time.*

When I arrived at work, I dried my soggy self off, fixed my hair and makeup and trudged to my desk looking poised and polished. *Nothing to see here. I'm fine.*

And yet a wave of utter hopelessness crashed over me as I sat down.

*Same shit. Different day.*

*There has to be more to life than this ... right?*

As I opened my emails, I noticed my fingers were trembling, that I had a knot in my stomach, and that I had an overwhelming feeling of dread ... like something bad was about to happen. Of course, I ignored it and pushed on.

Like every morning, among the mundane tasks sat the chaos. The 'shit hit the fan' moments that triggered the all-day scramble. I would fix, smooth over, shrink to keep the peace, find different solutions to keep the egos in check, rearrange timelines to suit the few, stretch resources, say yes to everything because saying no wasn't an option, people-please to do the right thing by others and always ... try to be perfect. *To prove I could cope.*

All at an unhealthy pace.

# BEGIN IT NOW

Endless back-to-back meetings with no real outcomes. Wasted time. Unclear strategies. Shifting visions. Power plays. Ego-driven micromanagement. All of it was wearing me down.

I was running on fumes.

I gave the best of me to the 116 change and transformation projects I was responsible for at work, while my family got what was left of me at the end of every 12 to 16-hour day. They didn't deserve that. I felt guilty. And ashamed.

I firmly believed that if I didn't work those long hours, I was lazy and unpromotable. I dreaded making mistakes, fearing I'd be judged as stupid. I made sure my work was perfect so I wouldn't be criticised! I was worried I was behind in life, not where I 'should' be. And I lived with the constant fear that someone would tap me on the shoulder to reveal that I wasn't as good as they thought I was when they hired me.

For over nine months - working overtime every day, including weekends, had become my reality.

This was not what I signed up for.

The feeling of overwhelm had crept in silently. I didn't notice it until that second meeting of the day, when I couldn't concentrate. Couldn't follow the conversation. Felt panicked. Anxious. Unwell. On the outside I looked composed. On the inside, I wanted to run away screaming.

I cancelled my next meeting and opened the Employee Assistance Program portal. It was now or never. I didn't feel prepared, but I also didn't want to break down in front of others. This was, as always, *inconvenient timing*.

Counsellor or psychologist? I struggled with this decision.

In the end, I based my choice on a psychologist with a kind face. Someone who could prescribe medication if needed. But mostly looked like someone I could connect with. That would listen. To hear me. To help fix me.

I got lucky. I got an appointment straight away.

The moment I walked into the office, I felt relief. I had chosen well. There was an immediate warmth, something I hadn't experienced in a while, and not long after, all the tears, bottled-up rage, and never-expressed-out-loud thoughts and feelings came tumbling out.

I wasn't alone.

They knew. They understood. Apparently, many people were feeling what I was feeling. There was a name for it.

Burnout.

An insidious, invisible shadow that creeps in silently. Envelops you in greyness, dulling your joy, your wonder, your aliveness.

Slowly. Quietly. It steals your confidence. Your inner peace and knowing. Instead it gifts you a persistent sense of overwhelm, self-doubt, feeling stuck and out of control, and a bone tiredness that sleep and rest can't resolve.

It was a relief to find out that I didn't need fixing because I wasn't broken. I didn't need medication either.

I desperately needed to find my way back to myself. To my dreams.

To my heart.

To the truth of who I am. To my power.

And that's exactly what I did.

I walked a tough but magical path of self-discovery and transformation. The gift this gave me? I found the quiet courage to begin yet again … and it changed my life. Priceless!

What had made me successful up to that point wasn't going to take me to where I wanted to go next. I had to unlearn. Old patterns. Limiting beliefs. The lies I had believed about success, worth and power. There wasn't an easy way. It was messy … and truthfully … it took a year.

Here's what I reclaimed and learned for myself:

My joy and inner peace: They are a choice, and if you have to give them up, it's too expensive. Always.

My voice and my values: Without them, you're steering your boat without a rudder. And you don't have to be loud to be impactful or heard.

My self-worth and self-love: What you reflect out is reflected back to you.

My confidence and inner strength: Without them, you operate from a place of lack and fear… and everything contracts.

My definition of success and what I stand for: Knowing this unequivocally helps me make decisions easily and intentionally choose the impact I want to have.

My right to rest, recharge, disconnect and unsubscribe from hustle culture: The productivity and laser focus you gain is next level. *You can let things be easy*. You have to experience this to believe it.

My authenticity and heart-centred way of leading: It's a powerful magnet.

And the biggest shifts?

The three months with my psychologist gave me the framework to become brutally honest with myself. To take radical ownership of my thoughts, my choices, my actions, my boundaries, my mindset, how I handle challenges, and how I speak to myself.

I had to continuously invest in myself and my own development to make what I'd learned sustainable. This is an ongoing journey.

Everything changed when I learned where to intentionally place my focus and energy, to prioritise what truly matters … above what is screaming loudest.

I learned to ask for help and found that this not only added value to my life but to the lives of those who helped too.

I gave myself permission to dream big. I had stopped believing the things I wanted were possible. I'm proving myself wrong every day. My vision for my life grows year on year.

I let go of perfection. It's impossible to achieve. Instead, I embraced the concepts of excellence and being *perfectly imperfect*. It's giving me a sense of freedom and fulfilment I can't describe. To be excellent like a ballerina, you need to make mistakes. Topple over to get the feedback you need to keep improving and master making it look easy. Without feedback you don't grow. There is a richness in gaining different perspectives that money can't buy.

I stopped making decisions solely with my head and started following my heart and intuition again. It revolutionised my decision-making and helps me stay true to myself. Finding my strength and trusting myself changed my life in the most unexpected, expansive and joyful ways; ways I never could have imagined.

Kindness. Real kindness was something I hadn't experienced in a long time. The heart in corporate seems to have been yanked out. *When did people just become cogs in a machine?* That moment in the psychologist's office, when someone saw me ... that kindness cracked me open. It gave me my mission. My purpose. My whole reason for having to arrive at that point in my life. Forty-eight years old, sobbing in front of a stranger saying; *'I'm not leaving until you help me fix myself.' They said only 1% of people recognise that they need to do the work to change. They are the successful ones. The rest want a magic wand.*

Now, at 56, I'm back in Australia with my family. I've spent the past four years building and growing my own coaching business, helping others do what I did: rise, remember who they are, and begin again - but from a place of power, not pressure.

If you've paid attention, you'll notice that between the ages of 48 and 56, I "began it now" a few more times. I moved countries. Again. Retrained. Again. Became certified as an executive coach and business coach. I moved from a stable corporate career and income into the adventures of entrepreneurship. None of it was easy ... but all of it worthwhile.

# BEGIN IT NOW

What I didn't know then but want you to know now, is just how good life can be when you finally choose yourself; when you stop waiting for permission, let go of what no longer fits in your life, and trust the quiet voice that says *there's something more or better meant for you.*

I couldn't have imagined the life I have now back then - a business built on purpose and heart, clients whose lives are changing as mine did. I could never have predicted the positive ripples this is creating, mornings with my family that feel slow and sacred, the sparkle of being seen and recognised for the work I once felt invisible doing. There's a softness in my days now. An intentional energy and power in how I lead. A clarity in how I live. I didn't just begin again, I began as *her;* the woman I was always meant to become and am still becoming. And I wouldn't trade it for anything. Following my heart and beginning again has been a powerful catalyst in my life.

I still face self-doubt, but now instead of shrinking or hiding, I choose to show up anyway. Just the way I am - messy and imperfect, with what I've got.

My life is wildly different to the one I woke up to on that rainy Monday morning in Auckland. It is one that is grounded in alignment and intention, and I love every inch of it. I'm still becoming. There is no destination on purpose. Only a vision and a journey. It's *my* life, and I can and do choose where I go.

This chapter is dedicated to my family who has always stood by me but especially my brother, who is currently living with Stage 4 cancer. It's incurable. He doesn't know if - or when - it will come back. That uncertainty lingers in every breath. And yet, every single day, he chooses life. He chooses beginning. No matter the hardship or difficulty that choice comes with on that day.

Together, we are proving every day that you are never too old to *Begin it Now* and that it's never too late to *Begin Again.*

As I'm learning to live and create my life the way I want it, he is faced with the fact that one day, he may lose the choice to begin again. And there lies the lesson.

The cost of not deciding is far greater than the discomfort of starting.

I could measure the cost of my own indecision, like the time I lost, the moments I missed, the pain I could have avoided ... but I choose not to. I forgive myself for not leaping sooner. For not knowing then what I know now.

What is your indecision costing you?

Don't rob yourself of the power to lead the life you desire. My wish for you is that you decide to do this for yourself ... sooner than I did. That you learn from my mistakes and get to where you want to be earlier. Unleash your magic because it's so needed in the world.

Here's what I know to be true now:

It's not that you're not ready.

It's that you're still hoping someone will give you permission.

We wait for a sign, some voice that says:

"Now's the time. You've got this."

No one's coming.

You give yourself the permission.

And clarity?

That comes *after* you move. Not before.

You can live boldly.

You can lead powerfully your way.

You can make an impact, change the world and leave your legacy. Without the burnout.

You just have to decide to *begin it now*. Or begin again. And again.

That power, what I call *the power to transform*, is already within you. Nobody can take that away from you. It's your choice.

Each ending is a beginning in disguise.

# BEGIN IT NOW

It's always a level up – even if you don't see it yet.

And just like a butterfly emerging from the cocoon, learning to spread its wings and fly for the first time, something beautiful is unfolding. It begins uncertainly, imperfectly and bravely. It's magical to watch.

So, just like the butterfly, take your heart, and your courage, and decide to *begin it now.* Not someday. Not when it's perfect. Not when you feel ready because that day never comes.

Begin It Now.

Because you are here.

You are worthy.

You can.

And your life is waiting to rise with you.

# SINJA HALLAM

Sinja Hallam, MBA, ACC is an Executive, Leadership & Personal Accredited Certified Coach (ACC) with the International Coaching Federation (ICF) and the CEO of The Power to Transform. She is also an international speaker and published author, award-winning change-maker, and the creator of the WiseHeartMind™ Leadership Method. A powerful, neuroscience-backed approach that integrates strategy, emotional intelligence, and conscious self-leadership. Her work empowers leaders to shift from survival mode into intentional, values-aligned influence of the kind that transforms lives, teams, and systems from the inside out.

With a dynamic background spanning over 25 years starting as a professional ballerina and moving through insurance, travel, organisational change, and senior leadership across mining, oil & gas, higher education, consulting, and banking, Sinja's story is one of constant reinvention. She understands change intimately, not just as a concept, and as a Prosci accredited Change Manager, but as a lived, embodied experience. Every pivot she's made, personal and professional, has shaped the coach and leader she is today.

Sinja works with high-performing women, and the men who

champion them, who are ambitious, driven and outwardly accomplished yet inwardly at a crossroads. Her clients are often navigating burnout, redundancy, career change, major life transitions along with

self-doubt, perfectionism, people-pleasing, or experiencing a quiet loss of self and confidence. Through deep, bespoke coaching containers, she helps them rewrite the internalised rules that have kept them over-functioning and guides them back to the calm confidence, clarity, and grounded power they were always meant to lead from.

Her mission is simple but radical:

To put the heart back into corporate.

Sinja believes heart-led leadership isn't soft. It's strategic. In an era of rising AI, relentless change and increasing performance culture, it's human-centred leadership that will define the future. When leaders choose heart, presence and values over velocity, they don't just thrive, they create the conditions for everyone around them to thrive and succeed, too.

Her work has been recognised globally:

- In April 2025, Sinja was awarded Silver in the Corporate & Public Sector Category at the Women Changing the World Awards in London.
- In August 2025, she featured on the TeamViewer F1 Academy Wildcard Car at the Dutch Grand Prix as part of the Visibility Drives Change campaign.
- She has been named a Top 15 Executive Coach in Adelaide by Influence Digest (2022 & 2024),
- She is a Senior Executive Contributor at Brainz Magazine and her thought leadership has also appeared in CEO Times, Fast Company, Glam Adelaide, and more.

# BEGIN IT NOW

Sinja is a trusted coach for leaders across Fortune 100 companies and mission-driven enterprises globally. She coaches in both English and German, and leads powerful workshops like The Rewrite: How to Lead Through Change and Thrive, a session designed to help people navigate the relentless pace of change, deal with the constant pressure effectively, redefine success, and lead with heart and influence to create environments for all to thrive in.

Whether she's working 1:1 through her signature Intentionally You program, guiding women inside The Power Within Collective™, or speaking to rooms full of changemakers, Sinja's message remains the same:

When we put heart back into power and power back into women, we change the world.

Website: sinjahallam.com
LinkedIn: linkedin.com/in/sinja-hallam-executive-coaching-global
Instagram: instagram.com/sinja_hallam
Facebook: facebook.com/sinja.hallam

# FROM SILENCE TO SHINING

## STELLA OLIVIA KIKOYO

**NO MORE SHRINKING: STAND IN YOUR POWER, SPEAK BOLDLY, SHINE YOUR LEGACY**

Your voice matters, Your courage ignites, Your light shapes the world.

*For God has not given us a spirit of fear, but of power and of love and of a sound mind. 2 Timothy 1.7* (**NKJV**)

For years, I lived in the shadows of my own life - quiet, agreeable … almost invisible.

I thought silence made me wise. I thought obedience equalled love.

But deep down, a whisper pulsed inside me: *You are meant for more.*

Over the years, that whisper grew louder. It was no longer a suggestion. It became a drumbeat. It became my call to rise.

My friend, this is the story of how I went from shrinking to shining, from hiding to leading, from silence to standing tall in my full divine power.

As you walk with me on my journey, I hope you hear your own whisper calling, too.

Because the world doesn't need you small – *it needs you whole.*

**GROWING UP IN THE SHADOWS OF SILENCE**

I grew up in Uganda; the firstborn girl in a family of eight. From my first steps, I was labelled quiet, shy, obedient - badges of honour for a 'good girl.'

At nine, after my mother's marriage ended, I went to live with my grandmother – my jajja. Mum threw herself into work, building the life that would one day allow me to become who I am. My jajja's house was never truly empty - often 8 to 10 uncles drifted through. My grandfather was mostly away. My cousin- the only other girl and closest in age, left after a while, leaving me mostly alone; a girl with my chores in a home where girls were not meant to dream big.

Evenings smelled of boiling cassava and shelled beans. Jajja's hands never rested. Watching her, I wondered – *Where was her joy? Did she dream of rest?* I was her shadow – braiding hair, singing, working, drinking endless tea. I loved her deeply, she was my world, but her house echoed the rules of another women's generation; work hard, stay quiet, keep dreams small. Inside me, a quiet ache whispered that life could be more - a life where a woman could laugh louder, move freer, speak boldly, and live beyond kitchen walls.

Outside, boys owned the world; climbing trees, playing football, roaming freely after their chores. Girls played briefly, then were called back inside for *more chores*. Commands rang out – 'Come here.' 'Girls don't behave that way.' By puberty, play vanished; life was simply school and chores. I longed for a place where girls could climb trees guilt-free, where laughter didn't end in work.

Inside, a kingdom of little kings ruled - uncles commanding, 'Fetch water!' 'Wash these plates!' Boys took chairs; girls sat on mats. Children stayed silent unless spoken to. I learned my thoughts were small, my words unnecessary. Without knowing it, I believed others' voices were worthier – a belief that chained me in silence into adulthood.

One day I dared to ask a question. 'Shhh!' The sound cut through the air like a whip, sometimes followed by a slap. So I folded my words inside.

But silence isn't emptiness. It plants seeds – stories, fire, power. I thought I was learning to be small, but I realise was gathering the fire to rise.

## THE KITCHEN PROPHECY

School was my escape, the one place my soul could breathe freely. I loved to study. My uncles, *my little kings*, sometimes helped with schoolwork, cheering my victories while reminding me *they* were in charge.

Home was humble but alive with love, until the day jajja's words shattered me.

I had just come home from school, eager to dive into my books, when she said, 'Even if you study hard, you'll end up in the kitchen. Even if you went up into the sky, you'd land back in the kitchen - where women belong.'

The last words hit me like a stone to my chest. I wanted to scream, *No, jajja! Not me! I am made for more! I do not belong in the kitchen!*

But I didn't. I swallowed it.

That night, staring at the ceiling, I whispered a vow to myself: *I will study. I will succeed. I will not stay in the kitchen.*

That whisper became my lullaby of defiance. Though silent, my little-girl heart was aligning with a greater truth; that a woman's voice and power were never meant to stay in the shadows. Somewhere deep inside, I sensed another world of possibilities - the same world I wished for jajja to see and live in.

Years later, jajja joined a women's empowerment group and started to encourage me to prioritise my schoolwork over house chores. Maybe, just maybe, books could lead a girl somewhere new.

**Key Lesson:** Silence can be both prison and sanctuary. What's buried inside – stories, pain, dreams – become the fire that fuels your rise.

Whispered defiance may burn quietly for years, but it holds the power to change everything.

## WHISPERS OF AN INVISIBLE GIRL – LEARNING TO LIVE UNSEEN

I became a people-pleaser; a silent shape-shifter- bending to fit the mould others carved for me. I listened more than I spoke, even when I knew the truth deep inside. Even when my words burned to escape.

Through school and university, my voice remained locked away. I sat in the front row, devoured knowledge and graduated top of my marketing class. In that achievement, I quietly fulfilled the first vow I made to myself. However, I never raised my hand. Fear was my shadow. I believed everyone else's voice was wiser, more worthy. Mine was invisible.

Then life dared me to step forward. I was invited to lecture at a top University Business School in Kampala, Uganda. Imagine that - the girl who never spoke, now teaching others.

Terror gripped me. My throat tightened. My heart thudded in my ears. *What if my voice shakes? What if I'm not enough?*

But my passion to teach burned brighter than my fear. I started small - practicing, stumbling, rising. Slowly, I learned to hold a classroom in the palm of my hand.

Triumph.

Yet in university meetings, my voice stayed trapped. My ideas remained locked behind my teeth – only to be spoken by someone else, who earned the applause that could have been mine.

I promised myself – *Next time, I'll speak.* But next time came and I stayed silent. Each swallowed word weighed heavier than the last. I felt the quiet slowly erasing me. Still, deep within, a spark was forming – a whisper that refused to die. I sensed the day would come when my voice would no longer stay silent.

# BEGIN IT NOW

## THE MOMENT THE CAGE CRACKED

After getting married, I moved to the UK to join my husband – motherhood, migration, a new life. I became a stay-at-home mum, haunted by my jajja's prophecy: *'You'll end up in the kitchen.'*

My accent. My background. My doubts. All whispered: *You are not enough.* Yet the desire to rise never died.

One day, I took a leap and applied for a lecturing role at London University. To my surprise, I was hired. People had said it wouldn't be possible. I was chosen to teach on the Chartered Institute of Marketing program – my dream. Fear almost made me decline. *Who was I to teach white British marketers?*

So, I built a mantra: *I am here because I have the expertise. My knowledge is valued.* It worked. My first classes were a success. Students celebrated me. The Institute commended me. Even my line manager said, *'I've never seen a class speak so highly of someone like this.'*

However, in staff meetings, my voice still hid. I continued to hand my power to everyone else.

Then came the day that changed everything. The meeting room buzzed – senior colleagues, flip charts, confident voices. On the screen, our department's biggest challenge glared back. And then - fireworks. A clear, simple, powerful idea lit up my mind.

I swallowed it. *Too simple. Too obvious. They're smarter. If it was worthy of being spoken, surely someone would have suggested it already.*

The chair asked for final input. I froze. Then someone I had casually shared the idea with spoke it aloud. The room lit up with nods, smiles, applause. Recognition that should have been mine, flowed to someone else.

*I felt betrayed by myself.*

After the meeting, a trusted colleague pulled me aside: 'Why didn't you speak up? This was your moment. You will never progress if you stay silent.'

Their words pierced me because they were true. I walked into the corridor, air cold against my burning face. Leaning against the wall, chest heaving, tears threatening - I broke.

Not polite. Not quiet. A bone-deep, soul-level cry rose from somewhere primal: *'NO MORE. NO. MORE.'*

Right there, I made a sacred vow: *No more hiding. No more shrinking. I will rise. I will speak. I will never again abandon the woman God created me to be.*

In that corridor, something holy stirred - *I am all that you need and here within.*

## ALL POWER IS WITHIN

And ... for the first time ... I felt the unshakable fire of my own voice.

**Key Lesson:** Your life shifts the moment you align with the truth. You have the Power. Courage isn't the absence of fear - it's the refusal to abandon your power ... ever again.

## PRIVATE VICTORY, PUBLIC POWER – WHEN INNER WORTH FINDS ITS VOICE

Months later, I attended the Chartered Institute of Marketing conference. Round tables gleamed under hotel lights, ambition buzzed in the air. Sharp suits leaned over notebooks, ideas bouncing like sparks.

In our breakout group where the task was to solve the Institute's challenge, the old voice returned: *'Stay quiet. Play small. Everyone here knows more. Don't embarrass yourself.'*

Two ideas burned in my chest. *Too simple,* I thought. *Too obvious.* The facilitator's bell rang - brainstorming over. Déjà vu. My corridor moment all over again; Stay silent and betray myself, or speak?

The vow from that cold corridor roared: *No more.* I inhaled, heart pounding, and words burst out: 'Wait - I need to say something!'

The table stilled. Every head turned. Face burning, hands trembling, I spoke. I shared my two raw, unpolished points.

Back in the main room, something extraordinary happened - every group echoed my ideas as key breakthroughs. The facilitator beamed: *'This ... this is exactly what we've been looking for.'*

Around my table, surprise. Respect. I felt fully seen. A rush of awe filled me. My private belief had met public voice - and that voice carried power.

For the first time, I saw it clearly - *I had always been enough.* The people I had placed on pedestals were just people. My voice was never small. It had only waited for me to believe in it and use it.

I walked out taller than I had ever been. The private victory of reclaiming my worth had ignited public power. My voice was now a force that could move rooms and shift outcomes.

**Key Lesson:** Your voice bridges who you are privately and the impact you make publicly. It doesn't just free you - it can influence, inspire and spark change. You were always enough. The moment you believe it; your whisper becomes power.

## FINDING MY STAGE: FROM SILENCE TO SHINING

After that conference, something inside me shifted forever. The silence that once held me captive was gone - broken for good. Suddenly, I saw myself in the world with a clarity and vision I had never glimpsed before. I was possible.

However, the journey wasn't over. I began to envision the woman I longed to be - a woman who could stand tall in any room. A woman who spoke with courage, lived with purpose and lit up the world with her brilliance.

I wanted other women like me to rise too - to claim their voices faster than I did, to lead, to shine, to step fully into their power. First, I had to become her myself.

So, I threw myself into the work. Coaching. Seminars. Workshops. Personal development. Books, NLP, Timeline Therapy. Layer by layer, I peeled away the fears that had kept me small. With every trembling step, I reclaimed my voice. With every step, I rose.

I launched *a women's empowerment group. I birthed Stellar Woman - the Magazine* and *The Stellar Woman Show – Podcast - I have interviewed powerful women like Sharon Lechter and Kim Kiyosaki.*

I have hosted global empowerment events, workshops, Stellar Table Talks – live streams and built *The Stellar Woman Academy*: spaces where women could thrive; where they could stand in their power and purpose, speak boldly, dream big, lead with brilliance and build legacies. I have sat on panels, moderates discussions and along the way, my work was honoured with awards.

I didn't wait to become fearless. I began afraid … and courage met me on the way. If I could rise from silence to speaking, from shrinking to shining, from hidden to whole – then so can you.

Here's the truth: *Your divine power has always been within you. Your voice is the key to unlocking it.*

**Key Lesson:** Your stage isn't a place - it's a choice. It begins the moment you show up fully as yourself. You don't need permission or for fear to vanish. Begin afraid and let courage catch you. Each time you speak your truth, you reclaim your divine power. When you rise, the world notices. When you shine, other women follow. Your stage is waiting. Take your step.

## THE RISE OF A STELLAR WOMAN – THE LEGACY OF BRAVERY

From the quiet corners of my life to the corridors of 'No More,' I shed silence and stepped into power, not just for myself, but for the women who would come after me.

Each time I found my voice, I was breaking the chains of fear for others, creating spaces where women could gather courage, speak their truth, and rise together.

Because when one woman chooses to shine, she lights the way for many more to follow.

## WHEN THE WORLD FINALLY HEARD ME – THE BOLDNESS NO ONE SAW COMING

My rise from shrinking to shining wasn't sudden, it was a journey of seven sacred soul shifts. Each was a quiet revolution, a step toward reclaiming my voice and power.

## THE SEVEN SHIFTS THAT UNLOCKED MY COURAGE:

- **Surrender the Need for Approval:** I released others' expectations: *'I only need my Creator's approval – I am enough.'*
- **Stop Dimming Your Light:** No more shrinking to make others comfortable: *'My light is unstoppable – I will shine anyway.'*
- **Speak, Even When It Shakes:** Fear tried to silence me, but I spoke anyway: *'I speak from love, not fear.'*
- **Drop Burdens That Aren't Yours:** I released generational pain and judgment: *'I release what was never mine to carry.'*
- **Release the Old You With Grace:** I honoured my smaller self and stepped beyond her limits: *'I step fully into who I am meant to be.'*
- **Choose Boldness Over Comfort:** Growth meant discomfort: *'I chose the road less travelled, even if it scares me.'*
- **Rewrite the Inner Script:** I took the pen: *'I am the author of my life. I write with power and purpose.'*

- **Exercise:** Pause. Hand over heart. Inhale your power, exhale your light. Whisper these affirmations and feel your courage rise. In this moment, you are at home in yourself. Your boldness is ready. The world awaits your voice.

## YOUR TURN TO RISE

If my journey whispers anything, let it be this: Your voice matters. Your presence shifts rooms. Your courage ignites legacies.

I was once the silent girl in the corridor, believing I wasn't enough. Now I know *I am because of the divine power within.* And so are you. Begin to stand in your power now!

## LESSONS I LEAVE IN YOUR HANDS:

**Your voice is your bridge.**

It connects who you are privately to the change you create publicly.

**Courage is a choice, not a feeling.**

Speak, even if it shakes. Act, even if it scares you.

**Legacy begins with a single brave act.**

Every 'No More' becomes a torch for someone else.

**Shining needs no permission.**

The world doesn't decide your light – you do.

**You were always enough.**

The moment you believe that, you unlock your divine power.

So here, at the end of my story and the beginning of yours … I place the torch in your hands.

Rise.

Shine.

And leave a legacy of bravery that will light the path for generations to come. STAND IN YOUR POWER NOW!

# STELLA OLIVIA KIKOYO

Stella Olivia Kikoyo is an award-winning visionary empowerment leader, Chartered Marketer, university lecturer, international speaker, and founder of The Stellar Woman Academy- a global platform helping women lead with purpose, rise with confidence, and build legacy-driven lives and brands.

Born and raised in Uganda and now based in the UK, Stella's journey bridges continents, cultures, and calling. Her life story is one of profound transformation: from navigating the quiet expectations of womanhood to becoming a bold voice of visibility and vision for women worldwide. As a mother of three and a wife, she understands the delicate balance between nurturing others and rising into one's own power and she helps women do the same.

As Editor-in-Chief of Stellar Woman Magazine and host of The Stellar Woman Show, Stellar Table Talks – Live streams, and global empowerment events like International Women's Day, Stella has created platforms that celebrate women's voices, inspire action, and amplify impact internationally. Through coaching, mentorship, and community-building, she empowers women to own their stories and step into their brilliance.

Stella also coaches for Street Business School, a global NGO empowering women in underserved communities to rise from poverty to prosperity. By training coaches who impact thousands, she helps create ripple-effect change that transforms families and futures.

Her thought leadership is amplified by interviews with global icons such as Kim Kiyosaki and Sharon Lechter, sharing stories of resilience, entrepreneurship, and purpose. Through a holistic hub of articles, expert features, videos, and real-life stories, she equips women to transform every area of life from mindset and inner healing to business growth and outward leadership.

Drawing on her expertise in branding, brand positioning, neuromarketing, strategic intervention, self-leadership, timeline therapy, and mindfulness, Stella works with purpose-driven coaches, consultants, and entrepreneurs to turn their message into movement and their identity into influence. Her signature approach aligns deep mission with practical strategy, helping women break through fear, dissolve limiting beliefs, design authentic brands, and build legacies that reflect both soul and strategy.

She has also expanded her impact into corporate training, delivering transformative programs in relationship-building, service excellence, and neuromarketing, equipping organisations to strengthen brand influence, elevate client experiences, and connect with audiences on a deeper, more human level.

Her global impact has been recognised with the Women Changing the World Award and as a Coach of the Year finalist, honouring her outstanding contribution to empowering women and transforming how they lead, live, and show up in the world. Whether speaking on international stages, training corporate teams, or mentoring one-to-one, her presence is empowering, enriching, and elevating.

Stella's message is clear: *"You are the one you have been gifted to be, so own it fully, stand in your truth, and honor all that has been entrusted to you.*

# BEGIN IT NOW

*This is your contribution to the world. Shine without apology."*

From Kampala to London, from grassroots communities to global stages, Stella Olivia Kikoyo is helping women and the organisations reclaim their power, rise into visibility, and create legacies that outlive them.

# MOUNTAINS OF LAUNDRY

## AN ENDLESS CYCLE

### SUSAN TOFT

I'm acutely aware of how fast time moves.

When I was 9 years old, my dad and my brother died in a car accident.

Dad was just 46 years old, the same age I am now as I write this. My son is now 11 and I often think about if history were to repeat itself, how different the trajectory of his life would become.

Tragedy, like what my family endured, makes you resilient in a way you can't explain unless you've been through it. When you've already experienced the worst that can happen and survived … your life takes a different approach. Every minute of every day, you know in your bones that life can change in an instant - and that we only get a short time on Earth.

This has shaped the way I live; always in a hurry, like time is running out. Always wanting to get to the next stage before it's too late. Always starting the next thing before finishing the last. Always jumping in to begin before I've worked out how to do it.

At 32, as a new mum, I was made redundant from my well-paid government job. The very next day, I picked up the keys to our new house. Overnight, our mortgage doubled and our income dropped by two-thirds.

The sensible solution would've been to get a new job. But the entrepreneurial spirit in me was waiting to catch fire. My dad had been an entrepreneur, quitting the family business as a cane farmer and buying a tenpin bowling centre. My career had been spent helping people build businesses. I knew I wanted to do this, but didn't yet have the idea.

It was during that time of financial uncertainty when I got the idea (my 'lightbulb moment'), walking past my spare room, looking at my clothes piled high, and thinking how I needed *a laundry lady*. By the end of that weekend, I'd decided that I should *become* The Laundry Lady. Before I had time to think about what that meant and how it would work, I'd jumped straight in. I had a friend create a logo and a website, registered the name … and The Laundry Lady was born.

It wasn't long before my solopreneurship took off - becoming the 'original' Laundry Lady servicing my local area. I'd gone from a corporate career sitting at a desk to picking up laundry and washing and ironing all day long. I couldn't have loved it more.

It wasn't the laundry I loved, it was the flexibility. The flexibility to work nights and have days with my son. The freedom to manage my own hours around childcare or school. Knowing that I could go to every sports day without pleading with a boss for time off.

The back-to-work as a new mum struggle was real, and I knew there'd be others out there who wanted the same freedom and flexibility. I had a vision that I'd scale the business, offering the same opportunity to others who needed to earn an income while having flexibility around their kids or life.

> *"If somebody offers you an amazing opportunity but you are not sure you can do it, say yes - then learn how to do it later"* Richard Branson

If I'd stopped and 'learnt' how to create a business first, I'd probably never have done it. My nature to dive straight in and work it out *as you go* was definitely a key to the business even starting.

I had no experience in creating a tech platform. I had no money to get started. I had no income. I had a baby at home. Despite supporting people to build businesses, I'd never started one myself. I just had a belief, deep in my heart, that this could be something I could build.

On a whim, I took a $5,000 budget to my 'tech' friend and asked for an uber-style platform. After his laughter died off, I came up with an MVP – a Minimal Viable Product, patching together off-the-shelf systems, just so I could get started.

People often ask me today what advice I would give to someone who is just starting out in business – and it's absolutely this: *it doesn't need to be perfect in the beginning.* Just get started. Work with what you've got. Find out if you have customers. Find out if it could work. The tech (in my case) or the detailed solution can come later. Just begin it now!

Building a business is a roller coaster journey. What you hear later as someone's 'overnight success' was likely 10 or more years in the making, with plenty of twists and turns along the way. You'll want to get off the roller coaster at every dip, but you'll also enjoy the ride, so much, that you'll have to stay.

But life is messy and gets in the way just when you don't want it to. Just as I got my MVP off the ground, I divorced and became a single mum. I had to restart my life with $40,000 of debt and no home.

I had to begin again.

After three years of putting my life back together, going back to work to make ends meet, erasing my debt and raising my boys ... there was another dip – COVID!

Another redundancy. But this time was different. This time, there was something in me that was ready. Ready to be all in. Ready to REALLY begin again.

The roller coaster took off and these last five years have been a wild ride; bringing on staff, moving into a warehouse, building the brand, going on NATIONAL TV to pitch on Shark Tank Australia, building one customer at a time … and growing the business to an 8-figure annual revenue!

And, most importantly, we now support hundreds (soon to be thousands) of people who were just like me, wanting freedom and flexibility in their working life. I'm so proud we are helping them all to … Begin it Now!

## WHAT I'VE LEARNT SO FAR …

### YOU DON'T KNOW WHAT YOU DON'T KNOW

We all think that someone else knows how to do it better, that someone who has gone through it before us has it all figured out. But the truth is, they were once where you are now. They didn't know how to get through it either. They just figured it out as they went. And you will too.

No one is coming to save you. No one will do it all for you. No one will be better at it than you. You are the only one who can do this. Remember the reason why you wanted to do it and figure it out on the way there.

### THERE IS NO SECRET TO SUCCESS

It's just persistence. Persisting every day – even when you feel like getting off the roller coaster and throwing up!

A few years ago, I hiked the famed Cradle Mountain Overland Track in Tasmania, Australia. 100km in one direction. No turning back. The only way out is to be airlifted. You carry all your own equipment, sleeping gear and food.

As I got out on that track, I couldn't help but wonder, "*What the hell was I thinking?"* I was unfit, I was overweight, I had plantar fasciitis foot pain – I'd never even hiked before. I kept wishing I'd booked the holiday to Bali to sit by a pool drinking cocktails instead. But for some reason, I set myself the challenge and off I went, with no turning back.

On the really hard days, (which, let's be honest, was every day) all I'd focus on was one foot in front of the other. *Don't look too far ahead and don't stop.* Just keep moving one step at a time.

Was I the last one to reach camp each day? *Absolutely.* But I got there in my own time. I got there!

There will be plenty of times, in business *and* in life, where you don't know what you're doing, or what's on the other side of the mountain. You just have to keep going and learn along the way. Focus on one step at a time.

## YOU'LL LEARN TO JUGGLE

As a single mum and a business owner growing an international business, my life constantly feels like a juggle. I've visited the hospital six times this year when my kids have injured themselves (life of a footy mum IYKYK). In my first ever board meeting, my son's school called to say he was sick (spoiler alert: he wasn't!). I've travelled a lot. I've pitched the business hundreds of times. I raised our first investment. I've started to scale the business into new countries.

It's a lot. *Every day is a lot.* People ask me how I 'balance' it all?

Well, I don't think there is any such thing as balance. Some days it's going to be all about work. Some days it's all about the kids. Some days it's all about both – and a billion other things pulling you in opposite directions.

What I've learnt is that whatever your life looks like, you'll be juggling plenty of balls. The key to juggling is to know that some of the balls you have in the air are made of plastic and some are made of glass. If you drop the plastic balls, they keep on bouncing. But drop the glass balls and they'll smash into a million pieces. You need to decide which are glass balls in your life and protect them at all costs. And the plastic balls? Well, sometimes you just need to let some of them bounce!

## YOU CAN'T DO IT ALL ALONE

Get help wherever you can. Maybe that's help at home. Maybe it's help at work. Maybe it's people helping you or finding the right tools or convenience. Maybe it's building a team. Whatever works for you, give yourself permission to do it!

For me, that's food deliveries, a cleaner, laundry pickup (thank you, Laundry Lady), a dog walker, dog groomer, my awesome Head Office team, AI tools, delegating chores to my kids, and my mum.

No one tells you that this entrepreneurial life will be lonely. Being an entrepreneur *and* a single mum? Lonely++. I'm not going to lie … I had a few years when the business was really starting to take off that were very lonely times. What got me out of that feeling was acceptance. Accepting that in this 'season' of my life, there will be lonely times. And accepting that being *alone* does not need to mean *lonely*. Sometimes just accepting the fact or changing the narrative in your head can make you feel so much better. It did for me!

And I've shaped my network to support my entrepreneurial journey, so that I never feel lonely. I've surrounded myself with an amazing network – my work team, women's networks, startup leaders, ecosystem supporters, tech leaders and mentors. Many have become close friends.

Everywhere I travel, I find someone in the room that I already know. If you've ever seen me speak at an event, you'll know that there is ALWAYS someone there from #teamsunshinecoast - this beautiful community in Queensland that I call home, filled with amazing supporters.

## CULTURE IS THE QUEEN

Culture is the powerful and guiding force that will shape everything you do. In my business, our culture is everything. From creating freedom for the people who join us, to the freedom we create for our customers, every part of that shapes how we work, how we think, how we interact, how we feel.

When it comes to our Head Office in Queensland, Australia, we've built a space that reflects our energy and values; a podcast pod where real conversations happen, neon lights that make you smile when you walk in, a lot of pink, and an awesome graffiti-style wall (who said a laundry had to be white!).

These are more than aesthetic choices. They tell our team, our contractors and our customers that we're not here to fit into someone else's mould. We're here to create something vibrant, authentic and unapologetically us.

We focus on life first in every decision we make. My team are not allowed to *ask* permission to take time off to get to their kids' sports days; they are *expected* to do it.

Our team work remotely and rarely see each other face-to-face. And yet when we come together once a year for our team retreat, it's like best friends getting together for a holiday. When a new person comes into our team, they quickly fit in like they were always there. That's the culture we've built. I can't help but smile when I see this happening in my team; this is so much more rewarding than hitting revenue targets.

I recently joined a team meeting online, a little late, and the team didn't realise I'd joined. Instead of interrupting their flow of conversation, I sat back and listened. I couldn't have been prouder of the way they interacted with each other, discussed the issues and made decisions that they felt confident were aligned with our mission. That is the culture we've built.

When your culture is this clear, this intentional, it doesn't just attract the right people, it empowers them to bring their whole selves to the table.

## BUILD SYSTEMS FOR FUTURE SCALE

Despite my chaotic nature, I actually love systems and have always been passionate about them throughout my life and career.

When I first began my business, back when it was just me working as the original Laundry Lady, I created systems every day. From the way I'd sort and wash the laundry, to how I invoiced customers, to the way I'd present the returned items. When I brought on my first contractors, those systems became their training. Today, that information has formed an extensive knowledge base for our global team.

When I wanted to create an Uber-style platform on my $5,000 budget (haha), I instead found an off-the-shelf platform that could do most of what I wanted. Was it perfect? Absolutely not. Did the business eventually outgrow that? For sure. But that 'system' helped our business grow to over $6million in revenue, to fully test the market and know that this business would work before we started to invest a lot more time and resources into building our own platform -TimeBoss.

Today, AI tools like ChatGPT and Claude are speeding ahead in their capabilities. I find that a quick conversation with Claude helps me create whatever new system or process I need at lightning speed … and with far less procrastination time.

Even if you are a team of one – whether you're a stay-at-home mum, an entrepreneur with a dream, or building a global business – think about creating systems simple enough to teach, but strong enough to scale. It needs to serve you now, and in the future.

## JUST GET STARTED

Seriously, what's the worst that can happen? Just get started and work it out on the way. You are never too old to get started.

I didn't start my business until I was 32. When life got in the way, I had to park it and didn't get back to restart it until I was 41. I've done it as a woman going through divorce. I've done it as a single mum. I've done it lonely. I have done it *broke*. But I've done it. And I'll keep doing it. Again and again. Every day.

Imagine a year from now, you look back on this moment. What would you wish you'd started now?

> *"Whatever you can do or dream you can, begin it. Boldness has genius, power and magic in it. Begin it now."* –William Hutchison Murray

I often stop and think about my dad at 46. If someone had told him the day he turned 46 that he wouldn't see another birthday, how would he have felt? What would he have changed? What hadn't he yet started?

My hope is that he would have said, 'nothing.'

# SUSAN TOFT

**W**hat could I do with an extra 5 hours in my week? It was this question – sparked while staring at the laundry pile mounting in her spare bedroom – that ignited Susan Toft's idea for The Laundry Lady.

Little did Susan know that streamlining a traditional household task like laundry using digital platforms would completely reshape an entire industry. And her own life.

Going back to 2012, Susan was juggling a demanding corporate career and motherhood, desperately needing more time for her kids AND a way to create flexible income opportunities for others facing the same struggle. What if she could solve both problems simultaneously?

It was more grit than glamour in those early days, but what started as a solo operation soon grew to 5 Laundry Ladies and Lads, then 20. These were real people – on-the-ground contractors earning meaningful money from home while completing washing and ironing for busy families, businesses, and aged care customers who needed their time back.

After 25 years in international marketing and business development with organisations like Austrade and PADI Asia Pacific, redundancy could have been a roadblock. Instead, Susan used it as the catalyst to hit reset on the business and give it her full-time attention.

Today, The Laundry Lady has over 400 contractors across Australia and New Zealand, with 90% being women who maintain complete flexibility around their family commitments while building successful businesses from home.

These include culturally and linguistically diverse women who've found economic empowerment through the platform, many earning substantial income while working around school hours and family responsibilities.

Laundry Lady is continuing to make big waves in the tech space with its proprietary TimeBoss® platform. By automating complex processes like contractor matching, route optimisation, and payment processing, they've made it easy for women to run successful enterprises without requiring extensive experience or capital investment.

Susan has created a marketplace where women and men can transform their washing machines into income generators, challenging outdated franchise models with authentic business ownership. Customers include residential, small business owners, plus the elderly and those living with a disability.

Thanks to its scalable tech, The Laundry Lady has scaled to an eight figure revenue business, while maintaining exceptional customer satisfaction. It has successfully expanded to New Zealand and secured investment for launch into Canada, the United Kingdom, and beyond!

Accolades include: Women in Digital's Founder of the Year 2024, Ausmumpreneur Awards Gold for B2B Service Business, plus Silver for Digital Innovation and Honourable Mention in Women's Champion. The company has also won Smart50 Awards, been named in AFR's Top 10 Most Innovative Companies, and reached the finals for Telstra's Embracing Innovation award.

These days, you'll find Susan sharing this story through speaking engagements, always with the message that flexibility isn't a nice-to-have, it's the future of work.

The Laundry Lady represents more than a successful business – it's a movement proving that innovation, empathy, and entrepreneurship can create solutions that genuinely change lives.

Those interested in Susan's story can connect with her at susantoft.com.au

# THIS BOOK CHANGES LIVES

Proceeds from the sale of this book go to creating empowered rural communities in Zimbabwe where all children have access to quality education regardless of their gender or socioeconomic backgrounds.

TTI's goal is to lead the development and growth of an improved education system, supported by socially engaged business models that boost local economies and enhance community livelihoods.

Aligning with the United Nations SDG goals for gender equality, Tererai Trent International Foundation is committed to creating a brighter future for women and girls and the whole community.

We believe that investing in women and girls is the most powerful way to change the world and these contributions provide opportunities for deserving women and girls to go to school, graduate secondary and even go to college, ending the cycle of early marriage, poverty and abuse.

You can read more about the work of Tererai Trent International Foundation and how they're changing the world here:

*Tererai.org*
*Tererai Trent International Foundation*

## ABOUT PEACE & KATY AND SPEAKING OPPORTUNITIES

Peace and Katy are the dynamic duo behind AusMumpreneur, Australia's number-one community for mums in business; Women Changing the World Press, amplifying the voices of thought leaders, female founders and women changing the world.

Peace Mitchell is a TEDx speaker, international keynote speaker, retreat facilitator and workshop presenter.

If you want your audience to be captivated by a heart-centred, warm and engaging thought leader and speaker then look no further.

With experience delivering keynote presentations on connection, business success, magic and productivity, there's nothing Peace loves more than engaging with your delegates to make your event a huge success.

If you've got an online or in-person event coming up and want to create a magical, warm and engaging atmosphere, please get in touch.

*peace@womensbusinesscollective.com*
*+61 431 615 107*

# ABOUT AUSMUMPRENEUR

Australia's number-one community for mumpreneurs. The AusMumpreneur Awards are a national event recognising and celebrating Australia's best and brightest mums in business. Held annually, these awards recognise the incredible women who are balancing business and motherhood and creating innovative, high-quality and remarkable brands across a range of industries.

*ausmumpreneur.com*

## ABOUT WOMEN CHANGING THE WORLD PRESS

Women Changing the World Press publishes thought leaders, female founders and women who are committed to making the world a better place through their words and actions. We believe that investing in women is the most powerful way to change the world and we are passionate about amplifying women's voices, stories and ideas and providing more opportunities for women to share their message with the world. If you have a story that the world needs to hear get in touch today.

*wcwpress.com*

## ABOUT WOMEN CHANGING THE WORLD AWARDS

The Women Changing the World Awards recognises, acknowledges and celebrates the trailblazers, changemakers and visionary action-takers. Providing a platform to amplify the achievements, accomplishments and work that women around the world are doing to make a difference in big and small ways. We believe that by elevating women, their ideas and their impact we can create a ripple effect that not only celebrates these women and the incredible work that they do but also inspires others to take action and make the world a better place in their own way too.

*wcwawards.com*

www.ingramcontent.com/pod-product-compliance
Lightning Source LLC
Chambersburg PA
CBHW071335080526
44587CB00017B/2849